Family Matters, Tribal Affairs

Volume 36

SUN TRACKS

An American Indian Literary Series

SERIES EDITOR

Ofelia Zepeda

EDITORIAL COMMITTEE

Vine Deloria, Jr.

Larry Evers

Joy Harjo

N. Scott Momaday

Emory Sekaquaptewa

Leslie Marmon Silko

Family Matters, Tribal Affairs

CARTER REVARD

The University of Arizona Press

TUCSON

The University of Arizona Press
© 1998 Carter Revard

⊗ This book is printed on acid-free, archival-quality paper.
Manufactured in the United States of America

03 02 01 00 99 98   6 5 4 3 2 1

Library of Congress Cataloging-in-Publication Data
Revard, Carter.
Family matters, tribal affairs / Carter Revard.
p. cm. — (Sun tracks ; v. 36)
Includes index.
ISBN 0-8165-1842-4 (alk. paper). — ISBN 0-8165-1843-2 (pbk. : alk. paper)
1. Revard, Carter—Family.   2. Indians of North America—Great
Plains—Social life and customs.   3. American literature—Indian
authors—History and criticism.   4. Indian authors—20th century—
Family relationships.   5. Indian authors—20th century—Biography.
6. Osage Indians.   I. Title.   II. Series.
PS501.S85   vol. 85a
[PS3568.E784]
810.8'0054 s—dc21
[814'.54] 97-21139
CIP

British Library Cataloguing-in-Publication Data
A catalogue record for this book is available from the British Library.

Publication of this book is made possible in part by the proceeds of a
permanent endowment created with the assistance of a Challenge
Grant from the National Endowment for the Humanities,
a federal agency.

These essays are for those who grow,
who build, who keep things working,
who have always helped and keep on helping—
Irish and Scotch-Irish, French and Osage and
Ponca, Comanche and Otoe and Lakota,
just to mention some in our immediate
families—for all the different beings, human
and other, who give good things and live
in good ways, our relatives and friends.
And you know, I kind of like Bill, and Hillary,
and Chelsea, and Socks, too.

Contents

Preface: A Word to the Wise

Some of these pieces have been published, most haven't. I've put them together because they make a community of words on Indian ground, good neighbors without fences, different and not always seeing things the same way, but cooperating when and where it matters. They are arranged in two sections. Those in "Family Matters" speak first of where I come from in Oklahoma, then of some later travels, and finally of where I live now. The first two tell something of what it was like growing up in a mixed-blood family in Buck Creek Valley on the Osage Reservation during the 1930s. The next one considers why and how I went to college. Then "Report to the Nation: Repossessing Europe" takes a slightly eccentric look at European culture in 1982 from one fairly Osage perspective; and the last piece, "Family Reunion," glances obliquely at a St. Louis visit by my younger brother and his kids in the 1990s, and tries to locate us in our present America.

The second section, "Tribal Affairs," looks from a more academic distance at what being Osage, or Apache, or Pawnee, or Taino, might once have been like, and at some ways in which American Indians now, with words, make places to live—in poems and novels and essays, as well as on reservations and in cities. "Making a Name" crystallized while I was spelunking through some dark parts of a course in the history of the English language, carrying as seed crystal my Osage name, and as with a geode the contents are colored by what seeps in from other springs, in this case bird-watching and place-naming interests. "History, Myth, and Identity among Osages and Other Peoples" grew out of my first efforts at teaching American Indian literature, working with such autobiographies as those of Geronimo and Charles Eastman, trying to learn all I could about the language and cultures of the Apache and Siouan peoples from whom they came. Part of this protracted wrestling with the Indian past was an effort to learn more about our people, the Osage. Having been given my Osage name when I was twenty-one years old, I discovered some ten years later the huge volumes of the Smithsonian Institution's *Bureau of American Ethnography Annual Reports* in which Osage ceremonies are transcribed and printed with translations by Francis La Flesche, himself son of an Omaha chief and speaker of Omaha (closely related to Osage), therefore able to talk with Osage elders about these ceremonies and be trusted by them to report them rightly. I have omitted from the present collection, however, my account of the Osage Naming Ceremony as La Flesche recorded it, "Traditional Osage Naming Ceremonies: Entering the Circle of Being." It is printed in *Recovering the Word*, edited by Arnold Krupat and Brian Swann (Berkeley: University of California Press, 1987).

As for the other essays in "Tribal Affairs," "Herbs of Healing," which sprang from teaching good poetry in my classes on American Indian Literature, evolved through presentation at a Modern Language Association (MLA) session, a public lecture given at the University of Oklahoma in spring 1989, and—in printed form— the "Native Heritage: American Indian Literature" issue of the *Nebraska English Journal* in 1993. "How Columbus Fell from the Sky" was commissioned by the Southwest Parks and Monuments Association for a 1992 volume edited by Randolph Jorgen, *Columbus and Beyond*, with essays from Paula Gunn Allen, Lee Francis III, Linda Hogan, Simon Ortiz, Ray A. Young Bear and me, in response to the Columbus Half-Millennium of that year. It was strengthened by my participation in a Washington University Faculty Seminar on Columbus with colleagues whose knowledge and edgy debate made it an interesting dream.

Maybe it would be useful to say, here, how I have come to study and write "professionally" about American Indian matters. My Yale

Ph.D. was in medieval English literature, my "fields" from 1956 to 1972 were Middle English and History of the English Language and Linguistics, with some attention to Computers and Natural Languages. For years, I made hardly any noises on campus about being Indian, and was not taken seriously if I did—or, as mentioned in the essay "Making a Name" in this collection, would find I had alienated myself, because I "don't look Indian."

Only about 1973 did I begin teaching courses at Washington University in which we studied the cultures and the literary work of Indian people—Vine Deloria, Leslie Marmon Silko, Scott Momaday, Charles Eastman, Black Elk, and Geronimo among others in the early going. It was hard work, and I had to learn all I could from books, from my Osage and Ponca folks, and from other Indian people I came to know. The teaching was at first in "extra" courses—outside the English Department and in addition to my full regular course-load—at the request of students or of administrative groups, and it began in part as response to sudden national and local interest in American Indian peoples awakened by the Trail of Broken Treaties and takeover of the Bureau of Indian Affairs Building in Washington, D.C., in 1972, and the Wounded Knee occupation of 1973. Both my Osage brother Addison Jump, Jr., and my Ponca cousin Carter Camp went on the 1972 Trail of Broken Treaties and fought in the Washington, D.C., action; and my cousin Carter was one of the leaders in the occupation of Wounded Knee (which lasted from February 27 to May 15 or so), so that some St. Louis radio and TV stations had asked me to speak or answer questions, on call-in shows, about those events. Now I had become an "interpreter"—now my "Indian connections" were suddenly useful, I could go out from the circled wagons and talk to the savages, maybe even assure them that *these* emigrants—immigrants?—were friendly and meant well. It's really funny, watching the readjustment of attitudes as "one of us" becomes "one of them"—ideas of what Indians really are might get shifted around. Since people are people, the shifts are likely more cosmetic than tectonic; deep changes might leave damages, as is no less true of me re-vising myself than of others re-viewing me.

After May 1973, while the U.S. Government was pursuing legal and illegal means of suppressing the American Indian Movement's efforts to get a more just and sensible relationship between Indian nations and the United States, people in the St. Louis Indian community began to get together. We held a meeting on the Washington University campus, early in 1974, and local Indian people were soon incorporating and finding a site for what became the American Indian Center of Mid-America. I met people I had no idea were living and working in the St. Louis area—Comanche, Apache, Kiowa, Cherokee, Seneca, Lakota, Omaha, Hopi, Mesquakie, Hidatsa, Otoe-Missouri, Navajo, Yaqui, Tohono O'odham, Dogrib, Delaware, Cheyenne, Chippewa, Arikawa among others. I could invite them to my classes to speak with real knowledge on Indian ways and Indian affairs, not only to tell us how the words in our books were pronounced, and some of the meanings above and beyond the usual glosses, but just as important, to show it was not just one "whiteface" teacher, but people who actually LOOK like Indians are "supposed to look," Real Redskins, still talking this way and doing these things.

And when our Indian Center began holding the first ever Plains Indian Powwows in St. Louis, from 1974 onward, I was asked to help in raising the funds, to be on the Powwow Committee, to provide contacts in Oklahoma with my Osage and Ponca folks and all the people they knew. Kiowa and Comanche people in the community started a Gourd Dancers group and asked me to become one of them, so for the first time I was not only attending powwows, as I had done now and then since I was a boy in Oklahoma going with my Osage and Ponca folks, but myself was dancing in the circle, was helping make the gourd and being given my blanket, bandolier, sash, ornaments, fan. It felt good, and strange, being "out there," and scary. I did not have that unspoken knowledge of powwow protocol, of tribal ways, that comes from having lived all the time with folks who know, who quietly understand what some camouflaged word or action means, how to behave, when to do things and when not. People in the community helped me, overlooked my mistakes or showed me the right ways, were kind and generous and willing to teach. I turned out to be a slow learner—for one thing, songs don't always get through my hearing aids, and at powwows I was sometimes at a real loss, had to let a vacant expression or smile cover my ignorance and hope it did not mark my stupidity. After a while, I could forget the anxiety and embarrassment and really enjoy the dances, even after I was elected to the AICMA Board of Directors and had to help organize and put the powwows on, with all the worries about the finances and the prizes and things like sound systems, setting up the arena and cedaring it, nailing down our arrangements for the drum and singers, head dancers, MC and arena director, schedule of events, camping places and firewood and food, giveaways, security people, all that has to be provided and managed and handled.

While I was beginning to learn such things, in the years 1971–77 people began asking me to publish some poems in journals and anthologies featuring American Indian writers. Fran Ringold, who knew me from my undergraduate days at the University of Tulsa and knew I was Osage, put several poems into a 1972 American Indian issue of her magazine *Nimrod*. After that, Larry Evers with the University of Arizona Press's Sun Tracks series, Kenneth Rosen for the Viking Press anthology *Voices of the Rainbow*, and Geary Hobson for his Red Earth Press collection *The Remembered Earth*, asked for new work and printed it. At the University of Oklahoma, Alan Velie had begun to teach a new course in American Indian Literature. In 1976 he and Norma Wilson, then writing her dissertation on Indian poetry, invited me to read poems there, and he printed some of them in his 1980 *American Indian Literature* (Oklahoma University Press, 1980). Through them I also met Frank Parman and Arn Henderson, whose Point Riders Press—then just getting started—printed *Ponca War Dancers* (1980) and *Cowboys and Indians, Christmas Shopping* (1992). When Norma began teaching at the University of South Dakota she invited me to speak during a 1979 conference there on Place and Identity, and when the *Denver Quarterly* asked me to contribute to a 1980 special issue of American Indian writing, I reworked the South Dakota talk into "History, Myth, and Identity among Osages and Other Peoples."

From the early 1970s, the MLA had taken note of the new writers and voices among American Indians, and Dexter Fisher and Lavonne Brown Ruoff and Larry Evers and Paula Gunn Allen and others

set up and invited participants to a National Endowment for the
Humanities seminar held at Flagstaff in 1977, from which a good
part of the scholarly work on American Indian Literature has sprung.
I was invited, but could not go because I had lately made some
discoveries in medieval English manuscript work that had to be followed up in England that summer (and many later seasons), so I
recommended my student Michael Castro, whose work in the seminar inspired his dissertation, which became the book *Interpreting
the American Indian*. The MLA invited me to serve on committees,
organize panel sessions, speak and read papers, facilitate publication of older American Indian books and texts, let the rest of the
profession know about this area. I met some of the great contemporary writers in this way—Simon Ortiz, Paula Gunn Allen, James
Welch, Scott Momaday, Maurice Kenny, Wendy Rose, Linda Hogan,
Joy Harjo, Luci Tapahonso, and Ofelia Zepeda among others—and I
heard some of them read the best poetry and give the best papers
at MLA sessions from 1977 through 1992. As I learned, I could
teach more and better; as publishers began getting these writers into
print, I could teach poems and novels as good as any of those being
read in "standard" courses: some of Wendy Rose's poems can stand
with those of Elizabeth Bishop; Simon Ortiz's with William Carlos
Williams's; the novels of Momaday, Silko, Welch, and Erdrich with
those of Pynchon and Elkin. When my own essays and poems began
to see print, the eyebrows of colleagues and friends here at Washington University came down a notch or two. Tolerance began to verge
on respect for the "new field." I printed, therefore I was.

I've had a good deal to learn, it is true, about how academic judgment operates, how many snobs think the publisher makes the poet,
the journal makes the professor, the university makes the scholar—
but it no longer surprises, though it still shocks me, if they "just
don't get it." I, in turn, can't see the point or the use of a lot of
contemporary writing which otherwise brilliant colleagues think is
marvelous stuff. My preference is for novels with plots, poems with
stories, and writers with a sense of connection to the people reading,
and I believe literature will only stay alive in the hearts of readers
who find it fills their needs, helps them laugh, cry, rejoice, under-

stand, and feel at home with those who put its words together for all of us. As Frost said, no tears in the writer, no tears in the reader.

True, there are different audiences, and some people actually find that John Ashbery wishes to destroy meaning and sorrow and love for the greater good of those few superior readers who can re-feel and re-word a universe in more profound Manhattanite ways; some of these readers find that Wallace Stevens, or Samuel Beckett, "really do it for them," as Luci Tapahonso's uncle said of Hills Brothers Coffee. So long as those people leave some star-country for Quincy Troupe, Wendy Rose, Simon Ortiz, I'm agreeable to their handing out divine reservations, or heavenly stars and garters, to their own tribes. What bothers me is when the publishers, prize-givers, academic raters, and all the Monoculturists insist on keeping literature white, European/New York/Los Angeles/San Francisco. What makes me reach for the swatter is horsefly committees and readers — even such astute readers as Helen Vendler — trying to tell me that Mr. X or Ms. Y is the great poet of this half-century, when they seem not even to know the work of the writers I have been teaching, because they read only certain journals, move in certain circles, listen to certain critics. But that only leaves it up to those of us who do read good literature that is "out of the main stream" (meaning, I suppose, it's like Lake Tahoe, or Crater Lake?) to get it across to other readers out there, so it can't so easily and smugly be ignored.

Eventually, I believe, whatever is well written is likely to be well read. No more is deserved. If people need it, they will probably find it. As for writers, I like something else Robert Frost said: "For I am There, / And what I would not part with, I have kept."

Acknowledgments

"Walking among the Stars" was first published in *I Tell You Now*, edited by Brian Swann and Arnold Krupat (Lincoln: University of Nebraska Press, 1987). "Report to the Nation: Repossessing Europe" appeared as "Report to the Nation: Reclaiming Europe" in the *American Indian Quarterly* and in *Earth Power Coming*, edited by Simon J. Ortiz (Tsaile, Arizona: Navajo Community College Press, 1984). "History, Myth, and Identity among Osages and Other Peoples" was printed in *Denver Quarterly* (1980), "How Columbus Fell from the Sky and Lighted Up Two Continents" in *Columbus and Beyond*, edited by Randolph Jorgen (Tucson: Southwest Parks and Monuments Association, 1992); "Herbs of Healing: American Values in American Indian Literature" in *Nebraska English Quarterly* (1993/4); a version of "Buck Creek: Time West" is here reprinted from *Prairie Schooner* by permission of the University of Nebraska Press. I am grateful for permission to reprint these pieces next to the new ones, where they belong.

A great help toward getting them written and revised was a May 1994 residency as Norma Millay Fellow at the Millay Colony for the Arts in Steepletop, New York. I am grateful to Francine Frank, President of its Board of Directors, for the fellowship, to Ann Lesser, its Executive Director, to the excellent staff and to fellow residents, for good times there when doe and fawn, wild turkey and coyote interceded with the muses for us, while snowmelt and rainwater sang alongside the road down to the post office. Walking and listening one day, I picked up from the stony road what I thought was a red-orange plastic lizard, which as it lay on my palm began to move slowly and was a salamander. When it was warm enough to keep going I set it down in the woods toward which it had been pointed, and when I came back up in an hour or so with my mail, it was gone. Thanks again, Ann and everybody, for transportation from snow to blossoms.

There are others who made it possible. For the amazing grace of a month in the Bellagio Study and Conference Center on Lake Como in October 1996, which let me finish the book, Stella and I offer heartfelt thanks to the Rockefeller Foundation's seraphim in New York and Bellagio. To Ofelia Zepeda, and Larry Evers, and Joanne O'Hare, for encouragement and support; and to colleagues, students, and administrators at Washington University, for a 1996 sabbatical, and good company, I am seriously grateful.

Then there are the people for whom these have been written— family, friends both Indian and other—and I would have liked to make them strong enough to be of interest to Benjamin DeMott, toward whose writing and whose example as teacher, man of letters, and man of conscience I look whenever I'm "weary of considerations."

PART ONE

Family Matters

Walking among the Stars

Right alongside the Osage County Courthouse in Pawhuska, Oklahoma, is a vacant lot that has been asphalted for the poor souls to park who have come in to face the music—for Driving Under the Influence, for bootlegging, assault, breaking and entering, marriage and alimony disasters, and (for that matter) for the foreclosures on sales and leases, I suppose, which those with property, vehicles, or spouses to offend with, or to law over, must come into a county courthouse and face up to. I'm told that in this waterproof blackness once stood a house rented by my grandfather not so long before I was born, where my uncles carried on a small but brisk business in bootleg whiskey which they bought wholesale down by Tulsa, from three Creek Indian brothers who (unlike most producers of white lightning) actually aged their product in charred whiteoak casks buried for several months or even a year. So my uncles always had a good market for the stuff they ferried up to Pawhuska in a Model A coupe with oversize springs, not just to bear the extra weight but so the car would not sag low enough to let the cops know it had a load of whiskey in it.

Before long, though, the police officers developed an informant network—or, as my Irish Uncle Woody put it, they paid some snitches to get in good with Osages who otherwise would never tell who sold them the whiskey. Eventually the snitches snitched on my uncles, and my grandfather—who never lied in his life, and would have nothing to do with lawbreaking, but couldn't keep his boys from getting up to such things—had to do thirty days in the county jail for it. The cops had come round to the house on evidence offered by the snitches, and although various uncles had rushed into the bathroom and busted the bottles and poured and flushed frantically, enough hard evidence was sopped up in rags to present in court. Uncle Woody, though—then about fifteen—had stashed some gallon jugs down behind foundation blocks, so the family could eat for the week needed to get a new batch of quality stuff. Never after that would the uncles rent a house in my grandfather's name: if a bust came, they'd be hit; he would not.

What's always agreed when this story's told is that there were no jobs around, so with no legal ways to eat, it was by quenching illegal thirsts that the DNA and RNA on this side of my genes could egg me on. There were, of course, people making an honest living in Pawhuska then. Just across that vacant courthouse lot, a back yard faced the house my folks called theirs—and in that yard stood the cultured, responsible mansion of the Mathews family, whose Osage son John Joseph Mathews had already been soldier (flying instructor in World War I), scholar (two years at Merton College and an Oxford degree), courtier (Paris, Morocco, Sunset Boulevard in the Roaring Twenties). He would soon return to Pawhuska and write *Wahkontah: The Osage and the White Man's Road*, and *Sundown*, classic accounts of what whiskey, cars, white sex, drugs, and invading legal lampreys, sliming through the spate of oil money, were doing to the Osages. The Mathews house still stands on Big Hill's brow next door to the old Osage Agency, a few steps from the new Osage Clinic where in 1981 I went with my Osage stepfather to beg anodynes for my mother, dying of cancer. Doctors don't lose their jobs, come recession or depression, just as bootleggers never lack for clientele—each making more work for the other, I guess. In 1978, when I brought some Indian Literature students down from St. Louis to Pawhuska, where my Osage folks gave a traditional dinner for them, John Joseph Mathews guided them and me around the Osage Museum that he had got funded, where the pictures hang of the Osage elders painted with the help of those funds—one picture, now, being that of Mathews himself—and we had some good words about our different days in Merton College, Oxford. (Jay Gatsby did not really get its library, where in fact the ghost of Duns Scotus still has the old book-chains to rattle.)

I think now of Grandpa Aleck Camp, looking out through the jail bars at the big house where maybe Jo Mathews was already writing, and my mother pregnant with my twin sister and me, looking one way at the Mathews house, the other at the jail. Did they wonder which way we'd go, if we lived? There was another man in the jail there about that time—the one who masterminded the murder of a good many Osages for their oil money, a story made into a novel later by Mathews's stepson, and again by the fine Chickasaw poet Linda Hogan (but please, reader, remember that her version is not necessarily Osage), and no doubt there are others yet to hit the keys. Now here those dead people are, looking out from these words at you. The past has windows, the future only doors, and God knows who may be looking at us through the peephole where in this ragged English I knock for some of us.

I guess I've happened because in 1930 among the customers of my uncles there were some mixed-bloods with lots to spend and lots of appetites to spend it on, and these apparently had an eye for beautiful nubile sisters of bootleggers, as witness my twin sister and me. Our father, whom I never recall seeing in person, died in the 1960s down in Texas, it is said, which is also where an uncle, a pretty well-known country-and-western singer whom I am supposed to resemble closely, once made his career. Twice unlucky, our mother did better the third time: she married our "fullblood Osage" stepfather Addison Jump, and we have four half-Osage brothers and sisters now. I was barely old enough to notice such things or remember them, but it must have been a wonderful change for my mother, moving from small marginal houses rented under the eyes and often the clubs of the law, first to the roomy modern house on Big Hill where we had a maid and a spaniel and a telephone and presently a new Pontiac Eight, and then from Pawhuska out twenty miles east to the Buck Creek Valley, the place where I grew up, five miles west of Bartlesville on an eighty-acre meadow with some tillable land, prime bluestem hay, and a Model B Ford pickup for use in farm work. The twelve-year-old house was wired for electricity with its own Kohler-plant generator; so was its two-story garage, with apartment space upstairs, its own cistern and well and inside bathroom working off water pumped from the well by a cranky two-cylinder engine in the motor house. There was a haybarn and stockbarn and windsock on a pole for the plane that the previous owners, before the oil money died in the Depression, had landed out behind the haybarn they used for a hangar. I sit typing this in the upstairs of the old garage, a fan drawing the ovenlike June air in somehow cool as I look east over knee-deep wildflowers and bluestem hay to the eastern prairie hills behind which Phillips Petroleum's research plant smokes, seethes, and sucks in hundreds of cars each morning, then spews them out each evening to trickle into Bartlesville or speed out U.S. 60 into Osage County. Did I say that Osage County is in fact the Osage Reservation, so I was born "on the rez" in the Agency town? Better stress that, for east-of-the-Hudson friends of the Indian who would like to know that a child of the wild who doesn't look much Indian (ah well, it's kept Hollywood away) was actually born on an Indian reservation and lived among the wild Osages when he was growing up. Did I say that the Phillips 66 oil company, whose world headquarters are in Bartlesville, Oklahoma, got its start in 1917 and still derives a little income from Osage oil, and that Uncle Frank Phillips, founder thereof, was an ol' Iowa farm boy who would give a big Sixty-Sixth Birthday Party for himself (just turned sixty-six years) and all the schoolchildren of the rural schools in Washington and Osage Counties? Have I mentioned that on the memorable occasion we children who attended Buck Creek (District 66) School in Osage County went in to this party at the old Bartlesville Civic Center, Uncle Frank came out on stage, between acts such as a basso singing "The Man with the BAY-AY-AY-AYSS . . . VI-*OHLL!*" and Gretchen Wienecke (later on Broadway in *Silk Stockings* as Gretchen Wyler) doing a sexy long-legged postpubescent dance? Uncle Frank told how he did it, worked hard, got up early, freely enterprised, started as a barber or maybe it was farm boy and then barber, always treated the Indians fairly, and we could do the same, so here for each of us was a sack of hard candy and fruit and a silver dollar.

But he did more than that for us children: he owned Woolaroc, down in the heart of the Osage Hills where there had always been a spring welling up, and he had bought several square miles of rolling blackjack-covered hills around that spring, dammed its hollow for a lake, built him a lodge, and brought back trophies from Africa—elephants, springboks, bongo antelopes, lions—and a skeleton of "an Indian who died on the Trail of Tears," and lots of wonderful things from the Spiro Indian Mound where he had bought digging rights. Better yet, Uncle Frank had live water buffaloes and American bison and wapiti and peacocks and swans and parrots and macaws and such, hanging and wandering around under blackjacks and post oaks, and I recall one school picnic at the end of the year, early May or so, when we were riding in the teacher's car, a redheaded lively woman who was replaced presently by a maybe too happily married woman who to the scandal of the board and neighborhood got pregnant and barely finished the year, my fourth grade, teaching us to add while giving us a practical example—well, when we were driving along the Woolaroc entrance road in the redheaded teacher's car, I was watching a group of wapiti of which one still had his antlers and just then his left antler fell off his head. It was hell getting them to believe me, but I pointed out that he still had only one antler, the right, and if anybody wanted to go over there the other antler would be lying on the ground. In those days, we said *laying*: it's a wonder somebody didn't say it might be *laying* on the ground but I was *lying* in the car.

So Frank Phillips helped to educate us in the Trail of Tears and the ways of elk antlers, but I never got the hang of founding a big oil company. So let us go back to Pawhuska to see what hung me up. A sense perhaps of impermanence, of being one of those who could be told to jump and cower for good reasons. Our houses did not last. When Uncle Woody and I drove down past the Osage Agency to the old Pawhuska cemetery to see the house where he remembered my being born, it was another vacant lot. "I be damned," he said, "it was right in here." It was one of those town margins, trees, the yards not exactly lawns, the grass that grows without being cultivated, where people work for others or they make a bare living or they never quite get the groceries paid for while they are trying to keep up with the other bills. So it was no surprise when we drove round the other end of Pawhuska, out where U.S. 60 leaves on its way to Uncle Frank's town, and saw a vacant lot where the old hospital had been, the one where we were able to do our small first wawling and crying (as Lear says) at being born. No surprise, but strange, to see it had melted into air, into thin air (as Prospero says), that second floor where we had run down the corridor and turned in to see my younger sister Ireta (Lay-dohn-wee-sa, her Osage name was), and my younger brother Jim (Akida Kihekah, Soldier Chief), and then Josephine, and finally Junior. These red bricks of the hospital had been so solid; our grandfather had hauled them up on contract, had helped build that hospital. The mules he had still used until about then were Old Beck and Jude, same ones who had pulled the covered wagon from Doniphan on the Current River in Missouri into the oil-booming Agency town of Pawhuska, after our Irish grandmother had died there in Doniphan.

All that work, the new brick town of Pawhuska my white grandfather had helped to build, the rented frame houses where we scuffed along. Vacant lots. Doctors, lawyers, merchant chiefs knew what— we, at their bidding, stood or sped. It was for the Agency and the Superintendent of it to say, later, when our stepfather was drawing some oil royalties, what must be done with oil money, and of course at first all of it was needed to buy the eighty acres, to put in the barbed-wire fence—driving the posts in with the big sixteen-pound maul, stretching the wire with rope and pulley so tight it twanged like a banjo and the post-staples screeked with the strain as we nailed the wire to the oaken posts. To dig the pond then, my stepfather Addison big and powerful, my grandfather Aleck short and masterful, the uncles swarming and laughing and swearing, the metal slip scraping and sleekly digging into the earth, grating into rocks that jerked and twisted the handles in my grandfather's hands as he held the slip on course and hyaahed the mules, and us barefooting in the slate-smooth track behind as the earth began being moist then muddy. Money went on a team of horses who died within a month, and on the pickup with which we dragged their corpses out behind the barn for the coyotes and the buzzards. We did not have to pay the buzzards to demonstrate flying techniques, their slow wheeling in Spencerian ovals across from the western hills and bluffs until they circled above our meadow, a quarter mile up, watching usurious from their naked red heads as they prepared to come down on a windy day, then tilting, slanting down, running out of updraft, sweeping and swinging almost out of control down to bring up braking, to drop short of the great bloating corpses, fold their wings like not quite reliable umbrellas—perching, lowering heads, picking, seizing, tearing, gobbling. But the *cattle* we had to buy, the *pigs*, the seed corn and seed barley, cowfeed, cottonseed cake! and with no threshing machine of our own, the neighbors to feed at the harvest dinner!

But we did have, now, a bluewater pond for cattle, and fish came into it, and willows began growing and elms and hackberries along its dam, and there were persimmons and buttonbush and such up in its swampy top areas where the redwing blackbirds perched and oiled their hinges and nested and complained and flaunted and sometimes were shot from the tall willow, now that it had grown all the way up, by my older brother who could hit a crow on an electric wire at a quarter mile with his singleshot .22, with Long Rifle cartridges at least. Yet this was a crazy bunch trying to farm in the middle of the Depression, with the uncles being killed by police or fellow bootleggers, all the stories of Uncle Carter getting shot when he came out of the bank he had just held up by police who had set him up with a snitch—entrapment it would be called today, but then they considered it a feather in the cop-cap; and about his being shot while hijacking a bootleg shipment coming in from Joplin— shot five times with that hideaway gun from the driver's boot, which Carter and his buddies had missed when they patted him down as they took over the stuff, while Carter was driving him off onto a side road to leave him there to walk back and tell his gang the whiskey was gone. And the much more guarded stories afterwards about what happened to the bootlegger with the hideaway gun, after he had been let off in court on a justifiable homicide—how someone nameless had followed that guy for two years and nearly got him in a little dusty town in Texas, but the guy got the wind up and skipped out just ahead, and finally that summer or late spring some years after Carter's funeral, word came that the killer was resting in peace.

And Cousin Roy who had sat across from the Pawhuska Courthouse with his squirrel rifle, him only thirteen years old, waiting for the cop to come out who had killed his dad, our Uncle Aubrey, the cop who beat Aubrey to death in the cell and then said he fell out of his bed and hit his head on the floor: the cop came out of the courthouse and Roy had him in the sights but just could not pull the trigger, and went to California the next week instead, hopped a freight with a buddy and landed in Truckee where he worked in a sawmill, then got into the migrant worker circuit with some other Okies that he knew from Pawhuska, worked the truck farms from lettuce down in the Imperial Valley up through the artichokes and tomatoes, olives and oranges in the Central Valley to the cherries and apples up in Washington, put the seedless grapes and tomatoes and lettuce on the tables of good old Uncle Frank and Uncle Winthrop and married a really good woman, smart, who saved up, and they had five kids, and bought them a used Airstream trailer after Roy got out of the Marines and they all worked with the kids chipping in and hell they got them a little land on the edge of Porterville and Roy built a house and put in a garden and fruit trees and there they were up in the edge of the Sierras and Roy could hunt him bears or deer or whatever and had half the year off to do as he pleased, go bass fishing, what Grandpa would have loved to do in Indian Territory no doubt if there'd been some honest way to do it and feed the family. And Roy saw to it that his mother came out and had a little house down the street with plenty of time and grandchildren, and there were oranges, apricots, loquats, cherries on the trees back there, tomatoes, okra, onions, peppers, in Roy's garden, rose trees and great crimson amaryllis blossoms by the front door—so far as I'm concerned he redeemed his time. So I'm glad he didn't shoot that cop, stayed that finger-squeeze away from a life in jail and gone to hell, and glad the freight trains were there for hoboes in those days, and glad there was a California before Steinbeck and Ronnie dumped the wrong myths into its margins. Frisco and L.A.

papers were still sneering at Okies when I was briefly semanticist-linguist on that Computers and Dictionaries Project funded by the Defense Department (ARPA in fact) at a Santa Monica think tank, and we could drive up to visit Roy and Celestine and their kids, when we lived in Pacific Palisades for that year and a half. I've put some words around Roy in a poem called "Okies" that's in *Ponca War Dancers*, and in another one called "Winning the Dust Bowl" that may get published sometime.

Well, so that isn't very Indian, is it? I should mention that Grandma Jump always had the cool quiet house with beautiful rugs and sofa and Indian blankets on the easy chairs and across the sofa-back, you know those Pendleton blankets all red and green and blue with their deep soft wool, so spirit-warming on a winter day. When my mother and stepfather got married, Osage oil money was still coming in, and his grandmother, Grandma St. John, was still alive, and she had some head-rights to oil money, as did his mother, Grandma Josephine Jump. So there was always fresh fruit on that big mahogany table in their dining room, and outside a big new Oldsmobile and a new pickup with camper canvas on it, and there were Aunt Arita and Uncle Kenneth who was a football player and boxer and went to Notre Dame briefly, just before World War II, and I vaguely recall when Uncle Louis (who was going to be a dentist in New Orleans and for whom my brother Louis James was named) drove too fast and was killed in a car crash. And Aunt Arita was smart, could type and do everything, and she read books, so my idea of Indians was not purely "Gettum up Scout" or "I will fight no more forever," let alone Twain's Injun Joe or the rest. There was always plenty of trouble and strife, but the most of it when I was a boy was on the wild Irish side and not the wild Osage. The summer after the war, I stayed over at Grandma Jump's to help Uncle Kenneth, still having bad dreams from the caves and foxholes of Iwo Jima, get the farm south of Pawhuska going again, and Aunt Arita had Marcel Proust's stuff around in a bookcase, and to get a break from shoveling oats one day I took a copy of *Swann's Way* into the outhouse and good old Proust would have sniffled if he had seen how the red wasp with blueblack wings, trapped in a black widow's web down in the toilet hole's semidarkness, interested me much more than *The Re-membrance of Things Past*. I have a little better sense now of what Proust was up to and may actually try to read the book one day. Not in an outhouse though—he still can't compete in that league.

But I had little sense, as a kid, how rough a time, and how wild and varied a time, Grandma Jump had had before I got here. Born in the 1890s, she was put into a convent school at ten and forced to speak only English. (All her life, she spoke with an Osage accent, though not until I was in college did I suddenly realize that that was what made her English run so counter to the usual cadences of pitch and stress; it was just the funny way she spoke, the "Indian" way, until in college I heard this guy who was a native speaker of Greek and his melodic runs were so different, it suddenly hit me: "Hey, you dummy, *Grandma* talks with a foreign accent!") Then at age four-teen, Grandma was married off by her folks to Jacob Jump (I am told this is a translation of an Osage name that refers to the buffalo jump-ing forward). So she had only four years of being taught English.

She was widowed after thirteen years, and had I think quite a life for the next twelve years, until her oldest son Addison mar-ried my mother. She was a strong woman, quiet but always know-ing what was on both sides as well as in front of her, and she had many friends in the tribe and was very much respected and lis-tened to. Photographs from her younger days show a tranquil, force-ful woman, handsome and unperturbed by the camera. She had a terrific laugh, loud and slow, which like her English speech rang the Osage changes, and it broke out oftenest for puns and word-play. My stepfather, her eldest son Addison, was born in 1910, soon after the Osages had been forced to accept individual allotment of their reservation lands, a time when the old ceremonies were being thrown away, as Francis La Flesche tells us in his transcription and translation of some of those ceremonies for the Smithsonian Insti-tution's *Bureau of American Ethnography Annual Reports*. So Addi-son was put into a military school, beaten if he spoke Osage, and had the language taken from him except for his understanding quite a lot of it. The younger children were educated, like him, in schools where Osage was being killed. So Grandma Jump's mother-in-law,

Grandma St. John, whom I knew for almost eight years before she died when I was ten (she was ninety, having been born on the Kansas reservation in 1851), barely spoke English; and Grandma Jump of the next generation was fluent in English but spoke with a strong Osage accent; and the third generation, my stepfather, uncle and aunt, had Osage peeled from their tongues and were left with English, only a little tangy with something which those who have grown up on the rez would recognize, even over the telephone, as an Indian accent on their Oklahoma English—and without the real Okie twang.

Grandma St. John, shorter and slighter than her daughter-in-law, was quiet too in the way of an Indian person, but when I knew her she seemed less queenly, maybe less imperial would be the phrase. I remember the time she came out to our place in the country, a year after my brother Jim was born I think (which might mean it was the ceremonial feast including corn planted to mark his naming the year before, if my understanding of the Osage Naming Ceremony is right), and she made some meat pies for us, a whole Indian feast with frybread and beef and corn soup I remember, and I loved the meat pies, which we had not had at home before.

By then the money at our place was almost gone, hard times were closing down on us. We had had a Pontiac the first year out there, new Buicks the two succeeding years; we had had a cook, a house full of new furniture and heavy window drapes that seemed regal to me, things trucked up from Tulsa, an expensive furniture store there, silverware and all, and always room for one or two or three uncles for whom there were still no jobs with wages, the house crammed and overflowing with children, so it seems. Then suddenly the money was gone, the Depression's dust was in our bowls, the long rainless baking summers dried up the pond, we sold off the cattle, the last Buick went sour though not till after its radio had brought us the Louis-Braddock fight. (I cheered for the Irish Braddock, then switched to Louis against Schmeling and always after that except for the Welsh Tommy Farr—must have been my uncles identifying with Celts.) We killed not only the pigs but the great sow, and Addison was having to work in the hayfields and hoeing corn and so were all of us boys, even Uncle Woody and Uncle Dwain

went out on the road selling magazines, the only job they could find
and lucky to get it. They drove a new '39 Ford from Brownsville,
Texas, to Butte, Montana, selling *McCall's, Newsweek, Redbook—*
postcards would come in, or letters from Butte on thin, quangly
sheets of copper, or a crate of grapefruit from Brownsville. But when
was it they and Uncles Arthur and Bert went out to Utah and worked
for the Mormons and had to do without coffee for breakfast with
those strict people there—as Uncle Dwain said, like to died every
morning? Twelve gallons of honey it was, I think, that they sent us
from Utah that time in gallon cans, lasted into school that fall, and
I learned to stir great tablespoons of honey into cold creamy Jersey
milk to eat with heavy yeasty rolls that our mother baked, hot and
dripping with honey and butter.

One thing was that with seven kids there were always plenty for
games, cowboys and Indians if nothing better—tree-climbing, swimming or fishing or hunting rabbits, squirrels, out on the meadow
or up in the hills around our valley after meat and adventure. And
when I was just old enough to appreciate the extra company, here
came our Ponca cousins—because Uncle Woody had met a Ponca
girl at the Osage Dances one year in September (they used to dance
in June AND in September), and by December they were married,
and presently there were Darlena and Buck and Carter Augustus and
Cordell and Craig and Casey. And because there were no jobs and
we had the Osage money in the early days, there would be weeks
and months even when Aunt Jewell and the Ponca cousins might
come stay with us, and later too when Uncle Woody was out on the
road, if he wasn't lying low avoiding a bootlegging rap. One reason
why, on the February day in 1973 when I read in the St. Louis newspaper that Indians had taken over the hamlet of Wounded Knee and
Carter Camp was serving as their spokesman, I was both worried
and proud, and a reason why I myself drove up there in March and
went inside to see what the hell was going on there, was that these
were my Ponca cousins that I grew up with running around the yard
or out in the haybarn or off along Buck Creek with. And another
reason was that before my mother had married Addison, Aunt Jewell and her Ponca folks had helped keep and raise me and my twin

sister down on the Ponca village at White Eagle for some time—the
first photograph of my twin sister and me, maybe a year old, has us
sitting in front of an Indian blanket, and was taken down there at
White Eagle when Aunt Jewell kept us there. I put one story from
that time into a poem called "Making a Name," first published in
Wanbli Ho at Sinte Gleska College on the Rosebud when Simon
Ortiz was editing it, and more recently in my 1992 *Cowboys and
Indians, Christmas Shopping*, which Frank Parman has published.

I don't have to say things, then—do I?—about extended families, and hard times shared, and a peculiar sense that being Indian
meant being very rich and very poor, quietly dignified and raucously
funny. I haven't even said anything about Uncle Gus McDonald, the
brother of Aunt Jewell and a traditional Ponca who had been sent on
his vision quest and was trained to be a Ponca leader, who became
a wonderful wardancer and was among those who first brought the
"fancy" wardance onto what I guess we can call the "powwow circuit." He gave you that sense of a man who was a great dancer, even
before he walked out there toward the drum and started to dance.
He could make you know this was a warrior, you could see what it
was that so impressed the Europeans, when they first arrived, in the
people who appeared to speak with them. It was a role: he stepped
through this door from 1491, came out with eagle wing and vision
to dance for us. But the dance was Gus—not all of him, but the way
light is not all of the sun, what you saw him by was this intense
brilliant presence. Besides, he was just one hell of a natural athlete;
as Uncle Woody tells it, Gus never lost a fifty-yard dash when they
were betting on him.

And his sister, Aunt Jewell, that little brisk-stepping woman I remember who could stand with her back to a wall and, bending,
put her hands back over her shoulders, flat-palmed on the wall, and
walk them down it to the floor and put those hands flat on the
floor behind her back, next to the wall (as I say of her in "An Eagle
Nation"). Even now, if you came along to a dance or a bingo night
down at White Eagle, I wouldn't have to tell you which was Aunt
Jewell—I've heard the Poncas say, laughing, you would know that
was Gus McDonald's sister, just from the way she holds herself. No,

not just a queen—every inch an Indian woman. And *laugh*—when did we all quit laughing, unless we were arguing or fighting? Or—well, yes, starving, like when all we had one Christmas to eat was some cowfeed and milk, and I am perfectly willing on the basis of that experiment to leave cowfeed to the cows.

Let's see, then. Earliest memories of small frame houses around the ragged edges of Pawhuska, of mules and uncles and homebrew and whiskey—then of the Ponca rez for a while, a time when Aunt Jewell and her great-aunt and her mother took care of us. Her aunt remembered when the Poncas were forced down from Nebraska into Oklahoma in the late 1870s in the time of Standing Bear (about whom in the late 1980s a movie would be made for which Aunt Jewell's daughter Casey Camp-Horinek would be a consultant, and her children and she would play bit roles in the trial of Standing Bear). I have written in "How the Songs Come Down" (in *Ponca War Dancers*) of the song we used to ask Aunt Jewell to sing us later, the Ponca song we could go to sleep unafraid with, and how it turned out that its Ponca words said, "What are you afraid of? No one can go around Death!" The aunt had made that song when, in Oklahoma, her brothers were so discouraged and the whiskey was getting the Poncas down so far, that she found this strongheart song, a warrior song to encourage them. Of her brother, Uncle Gus, I have written in "Ponca War Dancers," and of my uncles Carter, Arthur, Bert and Dwain as well as my grandfather Aleck Camp, in other poems printed in the 1980 volume *Ponca War Dancers*. I try now to think of each poem as a giveaway talk, one honoring that relative, the way at the end of a dance there will be a time when the Indians ask the MC to call up certain people, and the women will be given a shawl, the men a blanket, or some such gifts, and through the MC it will be told why the persons are being called to receive this. With good thoughts and a good heart, we tell of what this person has done that made us want to honor him or her, and of the good feelings that exist between our folks and this person. (Technically one does not call one's own relatives, so I play like it is the Muses that are calling them and I am just the MC telling what the Muses have given me to say.)

When I wrote "How the Songs Came Down," I was thinking of all

the places I had been, and of how each person is so like a black hole
out of which no light could ever emerge to another, and I began
writing thinking of how, there in the St. Louis suburban area where
I now live, I could lie at night and look northward out the bedroom
window into leaves lit by a full moon and streetlamp, new leaves
just softening all that light, and I could see a couple, fortyish, over-
weight, in Bermuda shorts and T-shirts walking down the midnight
center of the street below us, knowing we were up in our house
and knowing what we would have been doing but with no idea who
we were, who our folks were, what we were like as persons, and
ourselves no less ignorant of them, though they must be neighbors
living in the next block or two. Then there was a mockingbird singing out in the alley's catalpa just past our back yard, and I got to
wondering about a bird that would sing loudly at night when the
owls would be hunting by ear for such prey, and this began to get
together with the black hole thing, the way something in us sings
or shines out for the strangers, friend and foe, though in theory it
is not possible. So I was thinking too that it is not only people who
are so much in the dark to each other, but people and rocks, clouds,
trees, birds, all different creatures, and of how the memories in us
both stay and go, the way water stays and goes in a beaverpond with
the fish in it like our strange unseen theories and perceptions and
memories, time flowing like water through the dam of molecules in
our brain and "self" drifting there for a while. And how dangerous it
is to let out that foregathering of time, how at risk we are if we do
sing to the owls, like the mockingbirds.

But thinking that way I had a picture of us as kids in a summer
night under a full moon, those times before air conditioners when
we would go take our pallets out on the front porch in the moonlight
there in the Buck Creek meadow, and then how the radio shows
had once aired a series about werewolves, and the eerie howl over
the radio scared the scatology out of us kids, there under the full
moon and hearing the shriller coyote howls up on the hills around
our valley-floor meadow. So we were out there, and Aunt Jewell and
our Ponca cousins were with us, and Aunt Jewell sang us that Ponca
song as we were going to sleep, over and over. And I had heard

from Aunt Jewell, only a little time before writing the poem, what the words of that song say: "What are you afraid of? No one can go around Death!" And it struck me that this is how the songs come down, how we sing and let the owls listen, how Indian songs stay alive and help our people survive. So I was able to finish the poem and give her back some honor for the courage she gave us and still gives. But just so the Anglos don't think this is a song they should not listen to, or need not, I took a little swipe at old Willie Yeats in its last line, since I've always disliked his cold mechanical birds in Byzantium, and I cast Aunt Jewell in bronze there on our front porch, but a living bronze of American Indian—Ponca, that is. That way I was able to honor the mockingbird, our American singer that takes all the other songs and shouts them at the moon and to hell with the great horned owls, and honor Aunt Jewell when I said:

> She tells her children lately now, some of
> those real old things,
> now that the time has come
> to pass them on, and they are ready
> to make new places for what she
> would sing into
> the moonlit darkness like a
> bronze and lively bird.

If there are so many birds in the poems that come to me, it is because on the meadow and with the elm, catalpa, poplar trees around a house where birds would have only those trees except for the willows of the pond a quarter mile away, our trees were where the orchard orioles, robins, turtledoves, scissortails, bluebirds, kingbirds, dickcissels came to perch and sometimes nest and sing or shout. And the mockingbirds and shrikes, the indigo bunting (once) out in our garden, the yellow-headed blackbirds, flickers, redheaded woodpeckers and yellow-bellied sapsuckers, the meadowlarks flying and singing out over the meadow, landing twenty feet away from their sideways-tunnel nest down under the tall green hay and wildflowers so they could take a cautious periscope peek around before ducking under the grass and scuttling along their trails to the nest . . . and the bobwhites with their fifteen-egg nests, and sparrow hawks and the redtail, Swainson and red-shouldered hawks, the turkey vultures, the marsh hawks treasure-hunting low over the bluestem's meadow voles, rabbits, gophers and baby birds. How do kids in cities survive with only discos and videos and dope, broken glass in alleys and neat front lawns? For us there were baby rabbits that our cats would bring in stunned but alive, and skunks that educated our dogs but cats must have learned to let alone without getting sprayed, since I never saw a cat come sneaking and stinking in the way every one of our dogs, one time or another, did.

Sure, there were the dances, Osage and Ponca mainly—though not, for us kids, the way it was for uncles and older Indian relatives. Uncle Woody and Uncle Gus used to go roostering off in the Model A to one powwow where Gus would win the prize for the fancy wardance, then on to the next to repeat it; we kids never went along. It never occurred to me to learn the languages, words plentiful as passenger pigeons flying around the household in Ponca or Osage among the grownups—when Grandma St. John and Grandma Jump were there they always spoke Osage to each other, and Uncle Woody with the gift of tongues had learned fluent Ponca while he was hiding out from the Feds down at White Eagle, and Ponca was close enough to Osage that fluent speakers of either could quickly learn to hear past differences to the sames, so they could talk with my Osage folks. Woody was hiding down there that time when the U.S. Marshal, old Smithy Leahy, sent word along that he knew Woody was there and would be coming over to Pawhuska to his brother Carter's funeral—*but to come at night.* Uncle Woody did that, and sat up all night with the body, and went back to White Eagle without being arrested. Leahy knew Uncle Woody would get the message: Smithy would not have arrested a man at his brother's funeral, but he had some chickenshit deputies that would have done it and he could not control them during the day when they were on duty.

All those stories, all that language, all those times, passed over our heads and disappeared. Uncle Woody in the Aleutians during the Big War, later working for Rocketdyne in California, for the Atomic

Energy Commission at Hanford Plutonium in Washington (he had
to get Q Clearance, higher than Top Secret, to do the carpentry in
there, something that he thinks a long time later got him out of the
Plaquemines Parish Jail in New Orleans, but that's another story),
at Las Vegas (Lost Wages he calls it, and would love to live there), in
Porterville, California, fighting forest fires up above Los Angeles or
in the Sierras, his Ponca kids going to Haskell Indian School in Lawrence, Kansas, along with the Olympian Billy Mills, some of them
(as was my sister Ireta for a while) at Chilocco Indian School near
Ponca City.

So, like that mockingbird, I have more than one song, but they are
all our songs. It has seemed to me that no one else will sing them
unless I do, that when Ovid or Virgil or Horace promised someone
he would set them among the stars as long as the Latin language
should last it was not a bad idea, and it did not have to be some semi-
pro like Corinna that I'd fit with a constellation, nor even some
semi-thug like Octavius Augustus Caesar—it could be my grandfather, James Alexander Camp. When Octavius died he was holding
together pieces of an empire; when my grandfather went, he was
bringing in wood for our fireplace. My Uncle Augustus McDonald
was a better dancer than Augustus Caesar, or Nero for that matter,
and my cousin Carter Augustus Camp a better singer of Forty-Nine
Songs, not to mention he was once elected national head of the
American Indian Movement, and served the Ponca Tribal Council
by going to Washington, D.C., to confer with the then emperor's
satraps. Then too he and his sister Casey and their kids have been
working with that Maecenas-couple Ted Turner and Jane Fonda on
some fiber-optic epic or another, and who knows whether they'll
have their fingers on the button one day and wield more power than
that other Augustus. Somewhere, a kid on the rez. . . .

And schooling? The one-room country school a mile from home,
eight grades, my twin sister and I walking to it one spring to see
(I now see) whether we were up to starting it that fall although
just turned five in March. The long folding bench of maple wood
at the front of the room where the teacher held recitations—imagine eight grades, all subjects, kids from five years old to seventeen,

up to thirty of them, for a hundred and fifty dollars a month—
was smooth and comfortable, and we were up to the test, and at
thirteen she and I graduated as valedictorian and salutatorian after
serving as janitors during our eighth grade for the nine dollars a
month, which allowed us to contribute a little more at home than
just a pair of starving mouths. Good teachers, tough and tender Miss
Conner (herself Osage, her mother Mrs. Ridge being I think Cherokee) with whom we listened at noon to Bob Wills and his Texas
Playboys on KVOO from Cain's Ballroom in Tulsa; jovial avuncular
Mr. Loyd who hitchhiked from Bartlesville every morning that war
year of our eighth grade, played softball with and prayed over us,
harmonized beautifully on "Walking in a Winter Wonderland" with
a young woman from town who came out to the Christmas party
but would not marry him. Mr. Loyd's sister (Hazel?), though quieter,
shone with a nunlike joy, and even better when she came to visit
we knew the school meals might be breaded pork chops, cooked
better than any French chef could do them—well, maybe that two-
star man in Meaux, on the way from Paris to Brussels in 1964, who
had pity on us and let us in after hours (when our son Stephen, then
eight, looked at him with solemn blue eyes and said "C'est vraiment
fermé!" and the chef could not resist a little American kid speaking
real French)—maybe *he* could have made pork chops taste as good.

Ah well. Distinguished career at Buck Creek, spelling down the
school when I was in the third grade or so (with coaching from my
cousin Roy I admit—*have* to admit, he'd kill me otherwise), graduating as valedictorian of all Osage County (Reservation)—no, just
co-valedictorian, since Dicky Dickson of Indian Camp School in
Pawhuska and I tied for high total scores on five years of State Tests.
Then the shock of going in to Bartlesville Central High School's great
seething maelstrom of seventh-through-tenth-grade bodies brim-
ming with hot testosterone and estrogen, where I knew almost no
one but had the blessing of a twin sister to tell the girls that I was
better than I looked, and report to me which ones would not turn
me down flat. It was social limbo at first, not being one of the
poor defiant West Siders, nor rich insufferable South Siders—a real
Outsider. At age thirteen and very small for that age, up against it

with the boys but able to do enough kamikaze stuff in the lunch-time football games on the beaten grass and broken concrete, and enough country-style wrestling to keep from getting too badly bul-lied the first year. So unbelievably many girls had suddenly become so beautiful, I might have stepped out onto a Hollywood movie lot in that Sweater Girl time. Alas, no money for dates, no car, no line, had to get right back to the country every day to work after school, mostly then at training greyhounds—I hope there never is a place in any future life for cleaning out a hundred or so kennels of stink-ing hay, or raking the bones and crap, getting up at four-thirty or five in the morning and walking or running the dogs three to five miles before school, and after school cleaning kennels, grooming dogs, killing and skinning and butchering cattle and horses for them to eat, helping Johnny Kendall and his dad cut and stack firewood, plow and harrow the coursing fields for trial races. I loved the races, I very much liked the dogs, and it was great to go, in fall 1947, to the National Coursing Trials in Abilene, Kansas. All night drive to Wichita and on up to Abilene, a week of predawn breakfasts and feeding the dogs and walking and grooming them under the redden-ing skies and trying to learn secrets of dog-diet from rival grooms, psyching out the competition, spending a few nights at the skating rink and being treated as rich visiting celebrities by the local high school girls—what a change for Johnny Kendall and me! The Bartles-ville girls by then had us pegged as no mon, no fun; they would always be climbing out of some other guy's back seat and tucking in their blouses to go in for a malt and hamburger. So Abilene could've hooked me for life on betting if I had won a few more and had that kind of luck with girls on the proceeds, but luckily I failed to cover the touts at the trials when they offered a hundred to one against our white-and-brindle bitch Miss Border, who we thought would surely lose to the beautiful fawn bitch Frieda that had always outrun her in our Oklahoma trials—and Miss Border came out of the slips, sore foot and all, and beat Frieda up to the rabbit on the first turn by a yard, and outcoursed her like a neat little whippet. So when Miss Border killed the rabbit stylishly and cleanly with a single snap, and I ran over to clean the fuzz from her throat, snap the leash on her, and lead her out of the coursing park past the judges, who were dropping those red marbles down the winner's hole for Miss Border (instead of the white ones for Frieda), I was on the one hand dancing on air for our little winning bitch, but on the other thinking how to dodge what would be said to me by Mister Kendall for not at least putting up a couple dollars at those hundred-to-one odds offered just as I was going into the park with her to get her into the slips. Ah well, what he said was nothing to what my College Algebra teacher, Miss Villa Fender, said when I got back to Bartlesville College High School without the homework I had promised in order to be allowed to go to Abilene for that week. Still, it was worth getting the C that semester in math. And for some reason, gambling never got hold of me after that.

Very little Indian in high school except a beautiful Cherokee girl that picked somebody else, dammit. Senior year, they put me up to compete for a college scholarship in a couple of things and I won one, a kind of radio show, *Going to College*, that would now be classed as a trivia quiz, emceed by a brilliant speech and drama man from the University of Tulsa, Ben Henneke, later its president. This got me to the University of Tulsa. I won't drag through the standard college stuff here; there were good teachers, wonderful friends: Professors Eikenberry and Hayden, Ader and Alworth, Price and Tanner, Kaufman and Denekas and others, educated me so far as I was disciplined enough to get what was offered, and I ransacked the library and was given lots of books, and subscriptions to the best intellectual magazines—*Kenyon* and *Hudson* and *Sewanee* and *Partisan Review*, *The Nation*, *New Republic*, back issues of Cyril Connolly's little British magazine *Horizon* that had lately folded. I am embarrassed by remembering failures to learn, but for me they were the best teachers I could have found anywhere. They put me up for the Rhodes Scholarship and it was given to me. Then came the honor which is still the highest, along with the eagle feathers given me much later in St. Louis: Grandma Jump and the Osage elders and invited friends held a naming ceremony in September 1952 and gave me my name, in Pawhuska at the Legion Hall. Chief Paul Pitts, Mr. and Mrs. Wakon Iron, Hazel Lohah, the Ponca singers Francis

and Joseph Roy and Henry Jones and the Osage singer Morris Lookout, Harry Red Eagle, Mrs. Rose Hill, Mr. and Mrs. Henry Lookout
and Armeda Lookout, Jim Waters from Pawnee, Robert Warren Pitts,
Aunt Blanche Hardy and others signed the copy of Mathews's *Talking to the Moon*, which was given to me that night after the hand
games and all. A great kindness—and something more: after the
family song was sung (the Aiken song, put into the drum for him
when he was the interpreter and secretary to the Tribal Council),
when the blanket was put on me and we danced with many others
around the drum, we stood in place while everyone came past to
shake hands and to put money into my hands. Something about the
placing of those crumpled bills into my hand made me feel deeply
what it means to have a community, a people, tell a person: you are
one of us and we want to show you we support you, we wish you
well, we want your life to go well. A week later I was on a great
ocean liner, the first *Queen Elizabeth*, heaving and waltzing towards
England, and I still had those dollar bills in my billfold. When I took
one out to buy a cup of coffee in the lounge, or up on the deck, I remembered the people filing past me there in the Legion Hall, their
good wishes and good feelings as they spoke to me standing alongside my Osage folks there. Money never stays long in my pockets,
but that money stays in my heart.

So, sent to Oxford, I am reclaiming what's worthwhile in Europe
for our people, am calling the Muses to Oklahoma, where the cowpond we made is alive as those springs in Greece—of Apollo or the
Muses, Aphrodite or Athena—that in the spring of 1975 I drank from
with Stella and our children, climbing in and out of a little rented
Volkswagen beetle to refill our empty plastic liter-bottles as we clat-
tered up through the Pindus Mountains, then almost to the top of
Mount Olympus, all down the Vale of Tempe, past Ossa and Pelion
and the Triple Way, by sandy Ladon's lilied banks and through Arcadia to Olympia, and a last grove of blood-orange trees, to swim in
the blue Ionian Sea.

But I notice the Muses behave, over here, like the strong Indian
women they are—they sing Arcadian songs, in the Osage Hills, for

Okies to dance to. I'd like to bury Caesar, not keep on praising him.
The thousand-year Rome, thousand-year Reich, five-hundred-year
Ameropean empire are more than my meadowlarks can fly up to
the stars. And less than they want to fly with, since they need nest-
ing places in the Fifth World of nonaligned bluestem. I have tried
to turn the old stories, and new sciences, into present myth, in the
poem "Dancing with Dinosaurs" (in *Ponca War Dancers*). It is "science" that birds were once dinosaurs, science that some of them
migrate over the Atlantic from Maine to Venezuela, flying nonstop
at twenty-odd thousand feet for three days and nights. And I have
mythicized that the dinosaurs put on migration-wings only when
the continents separated and the new Atlantic Ocean came between
them and their winter homes. Then I have noticed that we Indians
put on feathers to survive, as the dinosaurs did, and that we sing as
the birds do, and I have raised this into a story that like the birds,
when we dance in our feathers to bring the new children into our
circle, when we sing the old songs, we are doing just what the old
Osage Naming Ceremonies, linked to our Creation Stories, describe:

> now as we face the drum
> and dance, shaking the gourds, . . .
> to honor on a sunbright day
> and in the moonbright night
> the little girl being brought in,
> becoming one of us,
> as once was done for me,
> for each of us who dance,
> I have called them here
> to set them into song
> who made their rainbow bodies long before
> we came to earth,
> *who learning song and flight became*
> *beings for whom the infinite sky*
> *and trackless ocean are a path to spring*—
> now they will sing, and we
> are dancing with them, here.

Into a star, the old singer sang, as he moved toward the House of Mystery where the child he would give its name was waiting among the assembled representatives of the clans, arranged to repeat the starry order: *Into a star you have cast yourself.* I am naming, as I go, as I approach the House of Mystery, those who have cast themselves into our stars and are walking with us here. I am Carter Revard, Nompehwahthe, at Buck Creek, Oklahoma, June 21, 1984.

Buck Creek Community

Time West

A half mile to our west, near where Buck Creek flowed under the U.S. 60 bridge, was where Toby and Joe Revard lived (cousins of mine), and they had horses to ride, old buckboards from before the Horseless Carriage, farm implements from Indian Territory time—horse-drawn mowers, seeders, plows—and a new Farmall H tractor. They knew the swimming holes and honey trees, would daringly walk pipelines high over Buck Creek; they would boost me to climb wild grapevines, light as I was, up to the sweetest clusters, or climb with us into old apple trees before grownups had come to pick the red ones. They showed us, on their Uncle Dewey's place, a labyrinth of wild plum thickets into which we could dive and scamper, stooping along bare twisty paths with tracks of maybe coyotes, cat tracks big enough for bobcats, and unmistakable skunk, possum, raccoon marks here and there, seen as we moved through the light shade-nets that made all the difference on a broiling summer's day, reaching up for ripe tart sand-plums and watching out for wasp-nests, bull-ants, centipedes. Some days if we timed it right and walked up to the Bockius house not long after their Aunt Mae Lewis had been baking, she'd give us something we liked even better to eat, her lemon meringue pies, or banana cream, coconut cream, pear or apple pie.

Sometimes their grandfather, old Guy Bockius, would be out on the wide airy east porch, playing solitaire. He had been a cowboy on the Cherokee Strip in the 1880s, and when he'd ride into Bartlesville for the big dances would win prizes for the best-dressed man and best dancer. And he was longheaded enough to ride over into the Osage Reservation and marry a fullblood wife, who shared the prizes with him. They had five kids who were half Osage, the last one (Jack) born just before the Osages finally were forced to accept allotment of their reservation land, which had been held in common, to individual families—so not only did Guy and his wife get their six hundred and some acres of allotted land, but each of their children also got his or her six hundred. They chose their allotments mostly in the Buck Creek Valley, starting from where the old Pawhuska trail came down into the valley on the west, then along to the north of that trail (it's now U.S. 60) toward Bartlesville for three miles or so. They ran cattle that grazed the deep bluestem hay into weedy stubble, grew Indian corn and wheat and watermelons in lush creekbottom loams, planted apricot and pear and apple trees and dug their deep wells down into cool sweet water, scooped out cattle ponds where the willow trees sprang up into tall dreamy sentinels. But with so much Osage oil money in the early days, they could mostly just live on the land and enjoy the barn dances and harvest dinners where hired hands would be bringing in the sheaves to threshing machines that roared and whooshed golden wheat-stems out their long galvanized spouts into tall soft pyramids of shining straw where we could climb and slip and slog to the top, then leap and slide cushiony-slick down over springy dusty looseness to fetch up half-buried in prickly straw over stubble and stickerweed where grasshoppers exploded around us in clouds of yellow and black and shocking pink wings.

Yet as Guy aged and his children grew into their own homes and families, Dewey and Della at the woods' edge to the north, Jack and Edith in bluestem meadow beneath the Big Rocks to the east, Short and for a while Dutch just southeast of Guy's home place, things were sliding downhill—the Depression hit, Guy began leasing some, then selling off a lot; the whole of it would go after his death to non-Indians, one an old cowboy, others mostly office

workers at Phillips Petroleum headquarters six miles east in Bartlesville, just over the line from the Osage Reservation. The long lush
valley and its surrounding wooded hills were first allotted, then
fenced off into sections, divided into smaller acreages and sold piece
by piece. In three generations it went from open Indian country to
mixed-blood ranches and farms and then to white commuter bed-
rooms. The third generation did no farming, let alone communal
harvesting or community schooling—its heart was the town, pulsing with jobs, churches, schools, banks, stores, people. World War II
came and went, machines took over, the rural school was put to
sleep to save commuters taxes, the valley's families ceased to know
each other, never worked or played or visited together, heard about
weather, crops, cattle, wildlife only from TV or radio. In the prime
time of the War's veterans, the valley became just a stretch of U.S.
highway past one county crossroad—grass, trees, houses of strangers
passing unnoticed while driving between towns.

  Guy's first-ever homestead acreage had been across Buck Creek
to the southwest, and later, when I was old enough to drive a tractor and plow and think about it, he was leasing out—to the farmer
who hired me to plow it—over a hundred acres of prime cropland
there, around the old wooden house in a grove of tall pecans with
its well of earth-cold water under a cedar's fragrance. Just before
World War II, my Ponca Aunt Jewell and my Irish Uncle Woody and
kids had rented this house for a year, and we kids would walk a
mile of an early morning over there to play with our Ponca cousins,
wading Buck Creek or crossing carefully on stepping stones that
were just upstream from the deep swimming hole. The steel-girdered
bridge over Buck Creek was being replaced that year, and we stayed
away whenever the dynamite blasting of its old foundations was
going on, then flocked in to marvel at the shattered blocks of concrete left below with their rusty iron rods sticking up out of the
water in drought time. Looking downstream at the deep hole, we
could see sometimes the big gars floating near the surface, occasionally putting their long sharp bills just out of the water and then
sinking, paddling on out of sight in the green-brown depths. Once
across, we'd clamber up the bank, where a little ditch-drain entered

Buck Creek there, and ease past that mass of morning-glory vines,
their tangle of sky-blue blossoms humming with bumblebees, in the
shadowless morning light leg-wrestling for golden pollen and prob-
ing deep for nectar.

The old homestead-house was then an unpainted four-room
shack, with a woodburning stove that Aunt Jewell could cook on
which almost kept them from freezing, that winter. Guy had lived
there for some years, near the turn of the century, when their children were being born. He was glad to rent the place, forty years
later, to my mother's brother, Uncle Woody, who had married my
Ponca Aunt Jewell a few years earlier. By then they had two little
kids, my cousins Darlena and Dwain, younger than we were but old
enough to go along with games of tag or hide-and-seek in the field of
tall Indian corn or to go swimming with their mom and us, though
being slow in learning to swim I only paddled around in the shallows that year. Uncle Woody was away mostly, a traveling salesman
for magazines, a job he'd got after leaving Pawhuska prone on the
back floor of a taxi, one step ahead of the Pawhuska cops that were
after him for bootlegging. He hid out for a while at our place, once
up in the attic over my mother's bedroom while the sheriff and his
deputy were questioning me and Grandpa in the back yard, again in
the summer of 1937 down in the woods along Buck Creek, surviving
partly by catching fish to cook over a small fire. My main memory
of that episode is the time my cousin Roy hooked and kept in play
for half an hour, on a rickety cane pole and heavy fishing twine,
the legendary Big Bass that lived in the deep hole downstream from
Gordon Wells, and how Uncle Woody came running to help, jump-
ing a barbed-wire fence in his haste, and grabbed the limber cane
pole that Roy was playing it on and tried to horse it out but broke the
line, to Roy's great disgust. Roy ran all the way up to our house to
tell us about it, so we piled in the pickup and drove jouncing down
the lanes and along back ways and then piled out and ran along to
his hideout, where Woody was sitting by his little fire, looking disgusted, with a pole and a broken line. Woody played it down as if it
was not much of a fish, but Roy swore it was the biggest bass he ever
saw, and he was already the champion bass-fishing kid in Oklahoma.

So we laughed but we looked into the long deep hole there and imagined it cruising with hooks and lines trailing from its mouth, and
to this day Roy swears about losing that bass. When he tells of it, he
speaks of the fish leaping high in a shower of rainbow drops, and no
fish of all he would ever catch could equal its magnificence.

But it must have been only a short while that Uncle Woody was
in the woods there, because my mother brought him a copy of the
Bartlesville paper with an advertisement calling for magazine sales-
men, and he sneaked up to our place by night and cleaned up nice
and went in and interviewed and out of who knows how many ap-
plicants he got the job and went on the road at once. A year later
he was in charge of a whole crew traveling in Texas, and presently
he handled crews in Minnesota, Wyoming, and Montana, selling
subscriptions and sending us postcards and grapefruit from Brownsville, Texas, Carlsbad Caverns, New Mexico, Butte, Montana, even
from Grandpa's old stomping grounds in Doniphan, Missouri. Uncle
Woody was six-foot-four and slender, with straight jet-black hair
and gray-blue eyes, had brains to spare, natural leadership, bound-
less energy, and must have kissed the Blarney Stone before he was
born. If he hadn't graduated from Pawhuska High School at the Depression's nadir when there were neither jobs nor colleges open for
bright smalltown kids with no money, he'd have ended up a professor or lawyer—and missed out on a life that surely, as he lived it,
was twenty times more varied and interesting than even a criminal
lawyer's might have been.

Sometimes when Uncle Woody was back off the road, Grandpa
and Uncle Bert or Arthur or Dwain would take us over in the pickup
to visit with him and Aunt Jewell. She reminded me, just lately, that
in those times we used to play horseshoes there, and then I remembered how fine-powdery-sandy the dirt was out in that yard; the
iron spikes we drove in as deep as we could but had to keep driving deeper because the horseshoes would keep digging away the soft
dirt around where they hit. The big cedar tree gave cool shade in
what must have been the dry late summer and fall of 1940, and Aunt
Jewell and Grandpa (then seventy years old) would pair off against a
couple of uncles, Bert or Dwain and Uncle Woody, and by that time

my twin sister and I were old enough to throw the horseshoes too
(they were real horseshoes, not those bought for the game in hard-
ware stores). It's a wonderful feeling to weigh and swing and let the
horseshoe fly, to watch its arc up and its turning over and over while
descending to clang and ring around the pole and stay there—and
so sickening to see it, as usually, hit just slightly off-balance and
go bouncing and rolling miles and miles away from the pole. The
competition is as fierce, the arguments as intense, the laughter as
sweet as in any game, and thinking about it I wonder why people
have to go to football or baseball games, and I think maybe it is because they don't have room around family homes, they have to play
in bigger groups, they need games which take more players—and
then as the cities grow they crowd in on families so much that not
only can you have no chickens or cows or whatever, you can't even
have room to throw a ball around without endangering neighbors or
their windows. And after a while you have to assign the playing to
others while you just watch, and then you farm out the rivalry and
hire professionals to do it all for you. And then you invent machines
which will bring you the pictures of the games and you are back
home again, only this time in your living room, or with one TV upstairs showing a basketball game, one downstairs or in a back bedroom showing a baseball, another a hockey game, another a football
game. And you go and get a drink of beer or cola, same flavor everywhere, made by professionals and cooled in a refrigerator hooked
into a great network of electric lines powered from coal mines in
West Virginia or Arizona, uranium mines in Africa or Australia, and
you maybe play video games powered by those same lines. Maybe
it is all a matter of how many people live how close together. Anyhow, there seems to be a lot less family game stuff now than in Buck
Creek times. Must be the demographics.

In our horseshoe games, Grandpa and Aunt Jewell usually won,
is how I remember it, but Uncle Bert had the most ringers maybe.
And then we could go back to the well, which had one of those
long tube-shaped galvanized-iron containers that you lowered on a
pulley-rope down the steel-sheathed well's tube like a subway car
to the water forty feet below. When you pulled it up again, the con-

tainer had a ring-catch trigger which you pulled to open and let its water come flooding out into a bucket. It was very cold and very sweet there under the cedar tree; the well must have tapped into the water table from Buck Creek only a hundred yards or so to the east, and never went dry even in the Dust Bowl years. I don't know when Guy Bockius had got that well drilled but I'd love to taste that living water again.

Of the water in that Buck Creek swimming hole though, my memories are not quite so favorable. As I said, I was slow learning to swim, and a couple of years later—after Aunt Jewell and the kids had gone up to Chicago with Uncle Woody for a while—I was camping out under the bridge there with my brother Antwine and our buddy Walter Parks, both good swimmers, and they were trying to teach me to swim in deep water. I thought I had got the trick of it and decided, while I was being ferried across by holding onto their shoulders, to let go and show I could swim the rest of the way—but promptly sank like a stone. I remember going slowly down through water turning dark and darker, seeing Antwine's hand come down out of the light amid bubbles and swirls and grab my hair, and saying to myself, *keep calm, don't fight, let him pull me on across and onto the bank.* I remember vividly that when I surfaced I reached out to put one hand on Antwine's right shoulder, the other hand on Walter's left shoulder, so they could tow me, saying again to myself, *keep calm, don't struggle, relax and let them pull me out.*

Unfortunately those memories are totally false, because after I had coughed and sputtered the water out of my lungs and nostrils, and was recovered enough to look at Walter and Antwine, I was amazed to see long red welts and scratches down both their sun-tanned backs, and I said, "What happened to you guys?" and they looked at me in amazement and said almost in unison, "What do you mean what happened to us? You nearly tore us to bits fighting when we were trying to pull you out," and Antwine said, "I almost just dropped you back in you were making it so hard to get you out." I swore passionately that I had been entirely passive and had kept telling myself to stay calm so they would not have trouble getting me out. Had their welts not proven they were telling the truth

I would never have believed them. From then on I have understood how witnesses or participants in such situations can give vivid, detailed, passionately believed and totally false testimony. And it took me two years before I'd swim in deep water again.

Guy Bockius had not lived long on that old homestead after the allotments were settled in 1907, I think, because after the great oil boom came in the teens, with each Osage headright worth a mint of money, Guy and his wife had got a big modern two-story home just up on the slope of the hill that we called Bockius's Hill, east of Buck Creek. Rising with the tide of black gold, they went all out—had gaslights in every room, a huge barn with hayloft, a two-car garage with apartment over it, roomy chicken-house of stone, storm cellar with cool storage space dug into the hillside (watermelon pickles and pear preserves in wild honey, green beans and beets and corn), with a big cistern for sweet rainwater beside the house and the S-shaped iron handle of the crank outside its green-painted cover to pump up the water in tin square cups, on that long bicycle-chain sequence, tipping and spilling into the cast-iron faucet where the jugs and buckets were filled.

Bockius's Hill was where the real woods began, the dense blackjack-oak forest of the Osage Hills on the west and north sides of our valley, where Buck Creek came down from western prairie and Doe Creek came down from northern prairie, meeting in a tangle of rich bottomland where Buck Creek turned south toward the highway. When my younger sisters Ireta and Josephine and brother Jim were a little older, after Toby and Joe had finished with Buck Creek School and were usually away from home, on a bright Saturday morning we would walk west, down past our pond, stoop through the barbed-wire fence and go on up that Hill and into its woods. We took fishing poles and worms for when we'd got over its ridge and down again to Buck Creek, but we mostly wanted, like the Bear Who Went Over The Mountain, to see what we could see—and maybe it was only the Other Side Of The Mountain, but it seemed a different kind of place, wild creatures not far away. There were some big rocks up there where we could look back into dark musky dens of maybe coyotes and bobcat, and much later, remembering this, and remem-

bering being caught up there in a thunderstorm once and having
to take shelter under one of the big rocks, I imagined one of those
dens as the place where a coyote pup was born and for the first time
heard a thunderstorm—and as the storm brought a chaos of sound
for the first time to that pup, there came also the sound of a little
stream near the den, changing its "tune," taking a different "key"
for it, which I imagined made the coyote realize that sounds could
become music, so the whole world was a different place from that
moment on, and I imagined that was why the coyotes would later
sing to the moon as once in a while we could hear them singing up
in those hills. I made a sonnet out of this when I was teaching at
Amherst College, and it was published in the *Massachusetts Review*
in 1960, the first poem I had written in my "Oklahoma" voice—so I
say that Coyote gave me my voice, and I made it the lead-off poem
in *Ponca War Dancers.*

In the earlier times, we had always hoped to hear old Guy talk
about his cowboying days, the more so because Toby and Joe had
shown us his guns while Guy was in Bartlesville with old cronies in
the pool hall down on Second Street, the Colt .45 from cowboy days,
a .22 pistol for varmints, the Winchester 30-30, and we saw they
were oiled and smooth of action. Toby hinted at the notches which
ought to have been carved in the Colt's handle, but Joe shook his
head and told him not to make that stuff up. None of us quite dared
ask old Guy directly to talk about the past or show us how he could
shoot. We had seen the dead coyotes and the red-shouldered hawks
strung up on barbed-wire gates where he had shot them. He was a
very friendly, very sociable man, direct and easy, liked to talk, and
yet we did not want to take any liberties around him.

But one lucky day, my buddy Walter Parks and I went over to see
Toby and Joe. They had just been told to go out to the henhouse and
gather the eggs for that day, so we went with them. They gave me a
small tin bucket (with hay in the bottom to place the eggs on so as
not to break) and I went over to the dim-lit row of nests from which
I was to gather eggs. There were more hens than nests, and some
nests only had a china egg in them (to encourage laying), but others
seemed to be favorites where several hens would lay, so five or ten

eggs might be gathered from one nest. But I ran into a problem: one old broody hen had decided these were *her* eggs, and no little stranger kid was going to take them away. I already had six eggs in the bucket, and I went up to her pretty confidently, but she fluffed herself up and glared and said *arrr* at me, fierce as a hen-hawk. I put out my hand to reach under her and take the eggs—the way she was sitting, it looked as if there was a whole nestful—but she pecked the back of my fingers twice, three times, before I could yank my hand back, and she put out her wings and made noises at me some more. So Toby came over and stood in front of her and poked a hand at her to distract her, and I reached a hand up slowly and quietly and slid it under her from behind and to the side on the nest. What I felt, under those warm feathers, was neither egg nor hen.

Instead, what I touched was rough-scaly and cool and, good God, *moving* slowly. Suddenly the hen leaped squawking off the nest and ran flapping and cackling toward the door, and on her nest, around and over the egg-clutch was coiled, oozing slowly sideways with tongue flickering, a long black snake. I snatched my hand back and yelled, and the snake moved quick as a thrown spear off the nest-row, down toward the wall. And then another hen leaped squawking from her nest, and we saw a second snake, as long or longer, thickly writhing away and down toward its companion, and we all yelled and ran out of the chicken-house at once, and Toby slammed and locked the door and jumped back away from it.

"Grandpa! get Grandpa, he'll shoot them!" Toby said. We set down our egg-buckets and ran up to the house, into the back door and through kitchen and living room and out onto the porch where old Guy was sitting, looking up cross-eyed from his solitaire layout (right eye looking at the bridge of his nose, left eye fixed unblinking on us, black as onyx), while Toby yammered about the two snakes. Guy put down the deck of cards, stood up and went inside to the stairs. We heard him climb deliberately up them and walk into his bedroom, heard a drawer open, heard him load both pistols and come back down the stairs, saw him turn and go in front of us back through living room and kitchen and out the back door. We followed him as he walked quickly but quietly along the hillside path to the chicken-house. He was carrying a long-barreled revolver in each hand, their muzzles pointing downward as he walked.

At the henhouse door he waited for Toby to come and open it for him. Toby reached up and swung down the wooden bar on its nail and carefully pulled the door open. Guy stepped over the sill and stood looking around while his eyes adjusted. We slipped inside just behind him. Walter was first to spot them. "Over there!" he said, pointing to a two-by-four wall-brace slanting up the far wall. We saw one of the snakes frozen along the brace with its head turned toward us, forked tongue wavering and whipping in and out. Midway down its six-foot length were two big bulges where it had swallowed eggs; that must have made the climbing tough. Guy raised the pistol in his right hand and we saw it was the .22. As he pointed it, the snake suddenly whipped round and flashed down the wall-brace, heading desperately for the floor, and Guy took a step sideways to get a better angle on it, and then there was a movement on the right-side wall and we saw the other snake hurling itself fluidly at the base of the wall, with a dry rustling sound on the concrete floor, hunting a hole. Guy must have decided he had a better shot at that one because he swung the gunbarrel toward it, aimed briefly and fired. He might have nicked it because it turned back, then darted desperately right towards us, and Guy shot again, and again—and then it occurred to us all at once that this was a cross-eyed man shooting in who knew what direction, the snakes writhing like rabid spaghetti and the gun swinging everwhichaway, and then Guy raised the .45 in his left hand and let fly at the first snake and blew its head off, which made it writhe and coil and whip round even more frantically, and all us boys tried to get out through the door at once while the .22 cracked and the .45 boomed and we didn't know whether we were going to get shot or crawled up by a big desperate blacksnake.

We did get outside and I slipped behind a big whiteoak. There were two more shots, both from the .45, a long minute of silence, then Guy called for Toby to come in. We peered in behind him and Guy had laid the guns on a shelf and was holding up a snake by the tail in each hand and they were longer than he was tall, kinking up along their length but their heads both blown off. One had swal-

lowed three eggs, the other only two. Later we decided it was pretty
good shooting there in the dim light with fast-moving targets but it
was agreed that next time we would have more sense than to go in
before it was over.

But we did not always make it as far as the Bockius house when
we set out to walk over there—not all the snakes and other distractions were in chicken-houses. Starting down through our bluestem
meadow, after we got past the blackberry patches where the cob-
blers came from and the cottontails would get away from our dogs,
we could follow the cowpath, almost bare, soft underfoot between
knee-high walls of green stemmy hay. White or lilac coneflowers
with bees on them, and wild sunflowers, nodded here and there
above the hay, with sometimes a goldfinch hanging on one brighter
than its petals; white larkspur, pink fluffy "prairie roses," brilliant
orange butterfly weed, lots of smaller milkweed were there for the
spicebush swallowtails, monarchs, sulfurs and tiger swallowtails.
Dickcissels chirred, grasshoppers leaped and spread orange or bright
yellow wings, green katydids clung to the stems. Snakes occasionally would half-appear oozing through the grass, or caught sunning
on the path would galvanize and zigzag out into the green depths
and disappear. At the back of our minds was always the dry shocking buzz of rattlesnakes—we had killed them at haying time, or on
the yard's meadow-edges, so our bare feet were slightly sensitive pat-
ting along that path. Besides, there were copperheads to remember.
Mostly though it was green snakes or hognosed snakes, sometimes a
coachwhip or long blacksnake, maybe a milk snake: lots of meadow
voles and baby rabbits, meadowlark and bobwhite nests with eggs,
grasshoppers and beetles.

And if we actually made it down through our meadow and through
the barbed-wire fence to walk along the pond-dam under its tall willows, we had the shade there, but also the water moccasins who
might be just down along the dam, where the willow leaves hid
their noses poking up, and sometimes they had crawled partway
up and would slide down and splash into the waters, and we would
watch carefully where we stepped going past. It was a big old pond
for ducks and sometimes at twilight a great blue heron, assorted

turtles, bass and perch and catfish, squishy mud and cool willow shade for swimming on an August day, legs treading cold depths and shoulders hot with sun—all sorts of things to learn. Once for several days we had held experiments as to which domestic creatures could swim, how far and how fast, the biggest surprise being that white leghorn roosters can swim quite well if thrown out into the middle of a pond, at least till their feathers get wet, and then you have to dive in and rescue them and see that they get dried out before going back to the hens and wondering what THAT was all about—looking much more warily at the boys next time they come by where the roosters are scratching up the ground and swaggering around feathering their favorites. And it turned out to be quite true also that a wet hen is just as mad as a man with no toilet paper (a successful earlier experiment on an uncle). Cats, on the other hand, do not get mad, they look terribly embarrassed and disgusted and betrayed after swimming horrified back to the bank, so I generally saw to it that our cats were well out of the way when the Bockius boys came over—they looked at cats just the way Tom Sawyer did, as creatures made for mean boyish pleasures. I had no difficulty protecting our cats, because they knew which boys would set dogs on them and which would kick the dogs away, so whenever I saw Toby and Joe heading over toward our house—there was always at least a quarter mile of warning time—the cats would follow me, or be carried, into the house or garage where whatever Bockius dogs were surging around could snuff and woof but not follow.

But Toby and Joe were much more than swimming instructors. If I never learned to ride bareback on a dapple-gray stallion in a rainstorm, as it ran full speed across the new-mown prairie and leaped that twenty-foot sheet of lucid water dimpling and bubbling with huge raindrops, my failure was hardly the fault of Toby Bockius. He did all he could to teach me, which was to holler "Hang on, here we go again!" and I surely did hang on, sitting—sort of—behind him on Stardust, my eight-year-old legs barely clinging atop his broad back, my rump lifting clear for each weightless moment as we flew over the puddle and I knew that next time I'd be looking up from the mud and water, IF I survived the fall.

Toby's name actually was Chetopah, or in the more scholarly way of writing it Tzi-To-Pah, "Four Lodges" (the honor-name of a chief of the Little Osages in the mid-nineteenth century who had taken four lodges of the Pawnee-maha during an attack), but I never knew who gave him the name, or when. My own name, Nom-peh-wah-the, "Makes-Afraid" (referring to Thunder's power, since my grandmother who gave it was of the Thunder clan) was not given me until 1952, and like Toby's was the name of a Little Osage chief around 1850–80,[1] so it seems that my Osage folks and his were related, and in fact he was of the Revards also on his father's side. Toby had some special relationship with gravity, not only on horseback but out on high precarious tree-limbs too. Sometimes if we did not go over to the Bockius house, they would come over to ours, and then we might go down to pick some plums or wild grapes at the southwest foot of our meadow where the great elms grew with a hackberry among them and the big grapevine was draped over one of the elms, not quite strong enough to bear the older boys but stout enough for me to pull up hand over hand into the lower limbs of its elm. Toby didn't need any grapevine: he put his hands and feet onto the hackberry's bole and went up like a telephone lineman, then swung and Tarzaned over into the elm. Ten feet or so from the ground the elm had a great horizontal limb that reached out over the meadow, nearly a foot thick and fifteen feet long before it branched and sent up tall columns of sawtoothed shady leaves where the robins sang reveille at dawn. And Toby would run along that limb with his arms spread out like a high-wire walker, shouting to me to come on as if I were just as athletic. He'd reach the first tall vertical branch and grab it, turn around and look surprised that I was standing there petrified, looking down at what seemed the faroff ground where the others were laughing at me. Ah, lightfooted Toby though, happy as the day was long and singing most of it, the way I remember him up to his early teens, he was just old enough to join the Navy in 1943, was shipped out to the South Pacific with almost seven hundred other sailors into the worst of that war down there, from which he and some sixty of his fellows made it back, Toby with never a wound on him. But when he got to be in his thirties he was laying block for a building high up on a scaffold, stepped wrong and fell eighteen feet through a hole; his back was broken and the wheelchair got him. Yet when I saw him and his brother Joe not long ago, at my brother Antwine's grave, Toby was as full of life as ever—he told me he is taking up flying an ultra-light machine, and gets around his eighty acres near Elgin, Kansas, in an ATV. I could see he still has the remembrance of things past to laugh about now and then.

Eastern Time: Buck Creek School

It was a one-room school with eight grades, a single overworked teacher handling up to thirty kids from ages five through about seventeen or eighteen—in those days a student was not automatically passed from one grade to the next, in fact a considerable number were failed and had to repeat grades, sometimes more than once. As far as I was concerned this was just fine, because when we were playing baseball against other country schools in the county (ours was Buck Creek Rural District No. 66), the big old boys who had failed several times in several grades, and at age seventeen or so were still in fifth grade, were our best home-run hitters and could go catch any ball hit to the outfield, or block home plate against any little pipsqueak smart kid who tried to score a run against Buck Creek. For some years I was one of our own pipsqueaks, always a year younger than other kids in my grade because in 1936, when my twin sister and I were only five years old, we were thought smart enough to start right into the first grade.

The school people had in fact looked us over before letting us start, it seems, because I remember very clearly the day Maxine and I were dressed in identical neat androgynous suits and taken—or, I seem to recall, we actually walked—that mile from our house to the school. It was a beautiful warm day, not hot, a spring day, early May I think, blue skies with white clouds, and I seem to recall every driveway we passed, each a quarter mile farther along. Only five houses at that time, white frame houses: Dave Ware's up at the corner of our meadow, then two houses facing each other across U.S. 60 another quarter mile along, then Tom Marshall's two-story Rocking Chair Ranch house just past the little bridge over Turkey Creek, then the Browns right across the road from Buck Creek School—itself at that time a small white frame building with a bell-steeple at its south end, a tiny two-room teacherage a few steps past that bell tower, two white outdoor privies down at the bottom of the three acres or so of school grounds, a huge whiteoak tree overlooking the concrete barrel-shaped storm cellar (with a wooden pull-up door and steps going down into its damp darkness) a few yards west of the school-house door. There was a tall shining slippery-slide and gymnastic rings and bar for exercise, and a set of six long dangly swings on their metal chains, with a merry-go-round that the big kids could push to dizzying speed or make go back and forth like a ship in a hurricane so the little kids could jump and practically fly as far as possible, competing to see who could jump the farthest without landing on the concrete storm cellar's top, or its native stone end-walls.

We almost always walked to school that way, but for some time that first fall a detour greatly changed things. They were building a new bridge over Turkey Creek—a mere gully most of the time, clear shallow pools and a trickle between them over flat sandy rocks—because the old bridge was narrow and dangerous. Cars had crashed into its unmarked concrete abutments more than once, and when finally a young couple were killed late one night, joy-riding out from Bartlesville at sixty miles an hour, the community rose up and demanded a wider crossing. But just as they got the old one torn down, and had placed the beams and girders ready for running the concrete body of the bridge, the rains came, and we knew there'd be trouble with the detour we had been using to the south, across a shallow pebbly place in Turkey Creek and up along old wagon-tracks to the back side of Buck Creek School.

It had been a Dust Bowl year, great wide cracks in the ground of our yard and meadow, a brown and stunted year for hay; we had greeted the rain with joy. But it kept up for days, what seems in memory like weeks, monsoon rains that soaked the ground until finally, up on the watersheds of Buck Creek and of that little Turkey Creek, there poured down what must have been a late-night cloudburst. In the gray early morning of that September day we could hear the roaring of Buck Creek in spate to our west, and over breakfast a conference determined that this day Uncle Woody would drive us to school in the Model B Ford pickup—neither my stepfather Addison nor Grandpa Aleck had ever learned to drive a car, Addison having said the hell with it after crashing the car he was learning in through a barbed-wire fence and being thrown through the windshield into the barbed-wire that slashed parallel scars along one side of his face, and Grandpa having also said to hell with it after the pickup he was learning in refused to stop when he said "Whoa!" and crashed into the back of our garage. Uncle Woody from his teen years had been one of Grandpa's designated drivers when they got an old Model T truck to haul bricks and lumber for the construction jobs in Pawhuska back in the twenties.

My mother had dressed Maxine and me up special, new light-colored twin outfits, faces scrubbed and hair slicked back, fancy new shoes, and we dashed out through the slow rain and piled into the pickup. Uncle Woody had stomped his feet into knee-length green rubber boots, figuring he might have to wade some. He was then just twenty-two, slim and wiry. He got us down through the deep ruts of our muddy lane and out onto the highway's pristine concrete, just laid down late that summer with Uncle Dwain as one of the highway workers who ran its concrete and filled its joints with hot tar (to his dying day he carried the big scar on his forearm where the boiling tar had got him once), and we chugged through the rain past the place where in August our cousin Roy had written his initials in the wet concrete. We could see ahead that Turkey Creek was up, but not high enough to be unpassable we thought, so Woody turned off onto the detour and jounced down the meadow's rock and mud and grass to the ford. It was brown and fairly swift and rising every minute as we looked, but having started only a couple of inches deep it looked to be no more than two feet now, so Uncle Woody shifted into second and we went roaring down the track that'd been cut into the bank, hit the water and slowed. Halfway across, the pickup sputtered, stalled, went dead. The water was up to and over the running boards, and rising; three tries failed to start the engine again.

"Here," Uncle Woody said without hesitation, "you kids let me get you on across, then you run on to school and I'll have to stay and push it out of the creek." He climbed out, stood on the running board while Maxine jumped into his arms, then he stepped down and waded on across to the school-side and set her down, and she started running toward the school, a quarter-mile or so away. Woody came back for me, sloshing and swearing, the water having got up over his boot-tops now. He plucked me out of the cab and carried me over and dropped me, saying, "Run like hell and you won't get so wet," and I started off as he was sloshing back. I did close the gap some on Maxine, but then I turned around and looked back to see how Uncle Woody was doing. He was in the middle of the stream, his back against the pickup's front, pushing and straining, slipping on the creekbed, but he had the pickup moving backward toward the bank. I turned and ran on, but slipped and fell headlong in a great muddy rutted patch of the track. I got up about as neat and clean as a pig from its wallow, and the rain began coming down heavier than ever and was streaming down my face, and I turned around and saw Woody had got the pickup back up onto the bank and was trying to start it. I started crying and yelling for Maxine to wait up, but she had got nearly to the schoolyard so I set out after her. It must have been the fastest she ever ran: usually I could outrun her, but that day she had wings and my feet were lead. As I neared the place to go into the schoolyard I saw her run into the teacher's arms, and be whisked through the door into Buck Creek School. Then the teacher came out, just as I ran up crying and muddy and mad, and she looked at me and laughed and laughed and said, "You look like a drowned rat. Come in and get cleaned up."

Buck Creek's schoolteacher for my first three years, Mrs. Fisher, was a woman full of life, whose husband I think worked way over at Pawnee while she stayed at times in the little white teacherage on the school grounds. She was redheaded, quick-moving, cheerful, never seeming tired or bored or unhappy. I remember that first spring day we had walked to school, Mrs. Fisher greeted Maxine and me, had us come in and sit down at a couple of vacant desks that must have been kept clear for us. It was a tough job, handling that many kids with no particular interest in the homework we were forced to do, yet Mrs. Fisher always seemed to be doing something extra, something requiring get-up-and-go. She drove her own car, and she drove it hard. She was in school early, well before classes took up at nine, got her work done and was out immediately at four P.M., disappearing in her neat little sedan toward Bartlesville some days, other days marching briskly out of the schoolhouse and into her little white teacherage.

But in the spring, when there was the big county-wide competition among all the schools held in the county seat, Pawhuska, and Buck Creek kids would be trying to win blue ribbons for singing, or playing instruments, or reciting speeches or dramatic things, Mrs. Fisher must have spent hours after school drilling and rehearsing and playing the piano for kids practicing. She also drove some of us all the way in to Bartlesville for "expression lessons" with Mrs. Camel (that was how her name was pronounced, but it may have been spelled Kammel or the like). That is, Mrs. Camel would have us read aloud, and learn by heart to recite "with expression." I have no memory of her face and form, yet I remember her voice, because at the end of my first year I was being coached to compete in the big Pawhuska competition, where I was supposed to recite *The Little Engine That Could*, and Mrs. Camel got me to be sure and do the part where it said "I . . . think . . . I . . . can" first very slowly, then slowly, then faster, then faster still, and I can still hear her voice changing from a straining near despair to a joyful belief and a delighted exulting speeding happy train's chuffing over the hill saying "I thought I could!" What I loved about her doing it was that in those days the steam engines did sound exactly like that when they started up from the Bartlesville train station. It was my first taste of onomatopoeia.

Her training went for nought in my case, though, because my understudy got to do the recitation. It was not that I was no good—everybody said it was magnificent, as I recall, though this memory may be as false as those when I had to be pulled out of Buck Creek—but that I hated getting up there and faking this. I did not believe in that little engine, I thought it was a silly story made up to get us to work on things we did not like doing, I thought that little engine was a Fauntleroy (now I think it is a hero and I wish I had not been so cynical!). But I got up there and dutifully practiced in front of our little school's kids, and it went all right, and finally we went over to Pawhuska, and we swarmed around outside with all the strange kids from all over Osage Reservation, having a great time and looking at the strange brick school and the houses with amazing flowers around them and going in to the enormous auditorium where there were fifty thousand strangers (well, maybe four hundred), all parents or competitors or teachers, waiting to see what we would do. And backstage, Mrs. Fisher said to me, knowing that I was not one bit enthusiastic about it, "Are you ready?" and I said, "I know it all by heart," and she said, "Do you really want to do it? You don't have to if you don't want to," and I said, "I don't really want to," and she said "Well, you know Joy could do it if you don't want to." Joy Todd was in the third grade, and as I look back I see it must have been that they thought this little five-year-old boy in the first grade would make a big hit, but just in case they had also prepared Joy Todd.

I remember Joy as a quick-voiced, happy and laughing girl, very friendly and likeable, the older sister of my rival and best friend Billy Todd (with whom I had fought a long recess battle to what each of us claimed was victory, I having backed him up with fists till he cried, he having kicked my shins black and blue). I remember Joy with greenish eyes and curly dark hair, a chunky build and a marvelously expressive face—she was more like Mary Lou Retton than Mary Lou herself. I remember in Buck Creek School both of us practicing on stage, and I thought she did it better than Mrs. Camel. Yet they had picked me to do the recitation, which must mean they had picked me over Joy, and I am guessing that this must have frosted the bra of Joy's mom, because I vaguely recall that when my mother and the Todds spoke backstage as the show was about to go on, there was a coolness there, and they had always been really friendly, our families liked each other more than most.

Anyhow, I looked at Mrs. Fisher and told her I just did not want to do it. She looked sorry and shook her head, but she called over to Joy and said "Carter doesn't want to do this, Joy, could you do it?" And Joy lit up like a Christmas tree, and she went smiling out on that stage and she knocked them dead—she won first prize out of all the rural schools of Osage County (which was Osage Reservation). It sank in on me, then, that I had refused to do something which would actually have been quite a good thing to do, and maybe I could have won that competition. Still, I was happy not to have done it, except that my mother seemed a little put out. It amazes me, in retrospect, that people left me so free to refuse, and made so little fuss over my not doing it. They must have been pretty decent people, Mrs. Fisher and my mother and all, to have done it so unharmfully, so casually that it did not bruise or rankle me.

The really pleasant part of that whole Pawhuska occasion in 1937 was my cousin Roy's winning his singing competition, which I think was what kept Mom from being put out about my missing the boat. Roy was eleven years old and in the fifth grade, a tough adventurous kid on the chubby side (then—but as a teen he was slim and powerful, joined the Marines in 1944 and fitted that uniform), warmhearted and sociable, street-smart and brave enough to do just about anything (nearly got himself drowned diving and swimming through an overflow pipe in the Pawhuska lake), but a great big brother type. He turned out to have a sweet tenor voice and Mrs. Fisher had put him into the competition for vocals. He was singing "I Love a Lassie, As Fair as Can Be," and nobody else was close to that good, so we were happy about the whole competition by the time we were driving home. His singing voice did not last when he grew up but his goodness did, partly because he married a smart and beautiful woman who's kept him good, so far. I talked about him in "Walking among the Stars," and in "Winning the Dust Bowl."

Roy was living with us that year because his dad had been beaten to death in the Pawhuska jail by a sadistic cop. His dad had done a fair amount of bootlegging, which would not necessarily have put him on the bad side of the police, who had plenty of bootlegging buddies, but Uncle Aubrey had a bad attitude. He thought the cops were mean hypocritical bullies, and they knew this was true, and they hated him for it. As Roy tells me the story, Uncle Aubrey was driving along Main Street with Roy and his mom and one of the cops I'll call Officer Keystone came over when he stopped at an intersection and said, "You're drunk, Camp, I'm going to take you in." To which Aubrey said, "I've had a drink but I'm not drunk, you can't arrest me when I'm driving okay," and Keystone said, "I'm taking you in by God," and Aubrey said, "You ain't hoss enough."

That was true, so Keystone called a squad car with three more cops, and they came and dragged Uncle Aubrey out of his car, clubbing him as they did, and pulled him into the cop car and drove him along to the jail. When they got him out of the car and tried to run him up the steps and into the jail, Uncle Aubrey grabbed hold of the railings and held on, yelling to passersby that they were taking him in to kill him. Roy tells me they beat his dad's arms black and blue getting him loose from the railings there; Roy says he saw it, having run along after the car and got there while they were beating on him, and Roy was crying and yelling names at the policemen there.

Once inside, the beating did not stop. Uncle Aubrey was taken out of the jail unconscious, and died without regaining consciousness. The official report, I have been told—admittedly I have never gone and looked it up if it still exists, so my account probably has a slight bias, having come from the son of the man involved—said he had been arrested while intoxicated, and in his cell had fallen off his bunk and hit his head, knocking him unconscious so, the officers were sorry to say, he died of a concussion resulting from his bad habits. I do recall Uncle Aubrey from earlier that summer, when I was three years old, and we had driven over to Pawhuska to visit him and his wife Loretta and our cousin Roy. It was a lovely evening, kids playing around outside the house and coming in as it got dusk, and once inside we had a dinner I recall only as plentiful, then some marvelous grapes that Aubrey and Loretta had got a whole case of, and then we kids did not want to leave and drive back all the way to Buck Creek twenty miles east (in those days the highway was dirt-and-gravel, the cars drove through the June dusk with windows open and you could hear the whippoorwills). So my twin sister and I had been playing with a big old teddy bear we had got for our birthday not long before, and we decided the bed we were playing on was to be a castle that no grownup could come onto, and Loretta went along with this for a while, and finally my mother and stepfather

Addison came in and tried to talk us into leaving, but we insisted no one could reach us and we were going to stay overnight with cousin Roy. At last my mother had to tell Aubrey to come get us, and he came in and played the stern judge and said we had to do what our mother told us, and then he actually got up onto the bed and reached over to get us one at a time, protesting bitterly, and with one twin under each arm went laughing out to the car and handed us in.

We have a lot of snapshots taken later that summer, after his funeral, when his brothers and our folks had gathered out at our Buck Creek house for a while, and my mother and stepfather had taken pictures of all of us with the big Kodak she had bought. The pictures were put into an album and when the house burned down it was rescued and my mother hung onto it and when she died it came on down and now is in my study. In the pictures Roy is at the house with us. His mother Loretta kept him with her in Pawhuska for a year, but then she decided to remarry, and when her second husband wanted to move to California and help run a sawmill and lumber operation out in Truckee, north of Lake Tahoe, Loretta and our mother talked it over and Roy—no fan of his new stepfather— came and stayed with us for a year and more while Jack and Loretta were getting things going in Truckee.

So that is why, my first year in Buck Creek School, my cousin Roy was there, and it was very lucky for me, because Roy was a great help in any way you could think of. He actually taught me to read, for instance—I remember the September day, home from Buck Creek School, when my twin sister and I sat in our living room, Roy with me and our older brother Antwine with her, and they ran a competition as to which of us, Maxine or I, could be the first to read aloud the whole page from that first reader we had been given. I remember the thick slick paper of the pages, the large letters those were, the slim quarto-sized book, I almost remember the words we were trying to spell through. We had been made to learn the alphabet, and learning to recite it had not been hard, but matching all the sounds to all the printed letters had taken more than a day, as I recall. And then they had given us the textbooks, and walking the mile home Roy told us we could learn to read the whole first story before the next day and Antwine said it would take us longer, because we were only first graders and it took them longer, as he knew from experience now that he was in second grade. But Roy said he would show Antwine that we could do it faster, and when we got home he would teach me and Antwine could teach Maxine. That got them to arguing who would teach faster.

So immediately once we got home Roy sat with me over on the big sofa—we called it a davenport—and Antwine with Maxine on a big easy chair, and we started trying to master the words and the sentences. My memory is no doubt lying, but the picture it brings is as clear as a Hasselblad would make those pages and their words, with Roy making me spell out each one, going word by word through several sentences, then going back and slowly getting fluent with one sentence, the next and the next. It was so intense I can't recall hearing Antwine and Maxine talking for a while, and then I heard them, and they were not as far along as we were. And then Roy pushed me to go ahead of where we were, and I could make out the next few words without him, or in a couple of cases with a helping hint or two. And in what must have been half an hour the whole of two pages, maybe ten or twelve lines to a page, was readable. And Roy called over to Antwine and insisted that now we had to show how far we had got, and Antwine and Maxine had not yet got through the first page, and so Roy declared we were winners. It seemed a great triumph, and it made Antwine mad as hell, and Maxine said it wasn't fair, and Roy fairly sang a victory song. I think that may have been as important a moment as any in my life for getting me into a literary life. And I grieve when I think of it, that Roy was already in the fifth grade and bound to have known better how to teach it than Antwine, only in the second, so Max got the short end of the stick. Had Antwine been Roy's age and vice versa, who knows whether Maxine would have been typing this and I would be somewhere, if alive, in a different life.

And then there was football and fighting that Roy mentored. At Buck Creek we had two fifteen-minute recesses a day—one at ten-thirty, the other at two-thirty—and we had the whole noon hour for lunch and playing. Recesses usually went for individual or small-group play—swings, merry-go-round, wrestling or slippery-slide or teasing and maybe fighting or whatever. But the noon recess in the fall very often went for football games, and there were enough boys to make two sides, each with what seemed then like huge numbers but could not have been more than eleven to a side and may have been eight or so. The age range being from five to about sixteen, each side had two or three big boys, three or four middlesized ones, and a rabble of little guys. The big boys regarded the little ones as nuisances and they ran over us or stiff-armed us any time they pleased. Some of the big boys were callous, others were kind, but Roy was chivalrous. He was not big, in my first year there, but he was a good size for his age, fleshy but not flabby—stronger than average, in fact, and dauntless. When he played football, he took no prisoners, but he went easy on the little guys. And he made sure when they were choosing up players that I was on his side, and he yelled encouragement whenever the action swirled in my direction.

We did not have a regular field, no lines marked, just put down caps or lunch boxes to mark the boundaries and the end zones. My first year, there'd been a new fence built, a heavy wire-mesh fence, across the east side of the school yard separating it from the oval driveway leading out to the highway. The fence was used as one end-zone boundary—to score a touchdown a player would have to carry the ball all the way up to the fence and touch the fence with the ball. To score a kicking point, the ball had to touch the fence on the fly. So the side defending the fence would try desperately to keep the other side from kicking or carrying the ball to touch the fence. That was how my one moment of glory in Buck Creek football came to pass, early in October of my first year there: as a shrimp on the fence-defenders' side, I was in the back row as the other side tried to kick a field goal on the last play before the noon recess was over. The kicker was Hobart Kahler, the biggest and strongest boy in school, and he kicked hell out of the ball so it came spinning end-over-end all the way over the heads of our big kids in front, and it would have hit the fence and scored a point for them—but I stuck out my arm and it slammed my arm up against the fence, bounced back onto the field, and was fallen on by Frank Baker for our side. Then the hassle

broke out: the other side claimed the ball had hit the fence. But Roy
had been just in front of me, had turned around and seen the ball hit
my arm and bounce off my arm not the fence. He testified, and vo-
ciferated, and showed them my arm turning black and blue on the
front and with red grid marks on the back from the fence, and they
had to give in, and we all went in for recess with Roy proclaiming
that his little cousin had won the game. Nobody took this seriously
but me, no doubt, but from then on I had no fear of the football
and when they would choose up sides they had no reason to leave
me out. So it probably was as helpful as anything that happened
that first year for getting me into the macho side of school without
great damage. I always hope there will be, for any given boy, a moment like that, early enough to make a difference. It only takes the
one time, I like to think, and probably somebody like Roy to raise
an ordinary event into one that really matters. Anybody who truly
wants to conduct a war on poverty and despair should find a few
people like him and sprinkle them among the families in trouble.

Sure, we spent more time in the schoolroom with books than
outside in games and fights, but character and status were cleared
up outside, in fistfights if necessary or desirable. Plenty of those
kids were vivid enough, and if this story was being told by one
of them the whole valley and its history would look very different. Or if I talked about Porky Starks instead of Toby Bockius, the
whole Indian-and-white-and-black balance would take a different
tilt. Porky Starks—Noah, to give his Christian name—arrived in
Buck Creek School the year I was in the fifth grade, when his folks
moved into Dave Ware's low-rent farmhouse down on Sand Creek,
where the Moodys had lived till then. Slender, not big but steely-
strong, "porky" in nothing but his nickname, he was Creek Indian,
black-bronze and with hair tight-curled on his scalp from the Afri-
can side back somewhere. He had a Greek god's profile and easy
smile, but fought anybody who called him nigger, which some of
the kids briefly did and long regretted. It took him about a week to
establish himself as the toughest kid in fifth and sixth grades, somebody not even the big boys would mess with, the way a grizzly won't

mess with a wolverine. Though he never seemed to start the fights, when I remember how they broke out I think Porky got them to happen, knew they were necessary or useful. Each time was like a Demolition Derby—he never swerved from expected collisions and always left the other guy disabled.

Porky and my brother Antwine became best friends, got through Buck Creek together then dropped out of school, and even when the Starks moved away that year Porky would come by and stay overnight now and then, and Antwine would just as often get over to Pawhuska or wherever Porky was living. By sixteen, Porky was right at six feet tall, a hundred and seventy pounds of spring steel with a deep easy laugh and his choice of women. Antwine and he were hanging out with some of the roughest guys in Pawhuska by that time, and for a couple of years there was only one other guy, an Osage mixed-blood who hit those same honkytonks, that was thought to be Porky's equal maybe, and we expected that one Saturday night they would show up in the same place and maybe tear it down in a title fight, but that never happened. I ran with a different bunch (Cokes and skating rinks, not bourbon and beerjoints), so I missed the action, but got reports from eyewitnesses (my old buddy Walter Parks for one) who spoke in awe of big bruisers dismantled, of women running over to the car windows to ask for a ride with Porky and his having to fight their boyfriends, two or three in an evening it seemed. The night somebody got an ear bit off on a Pawhuska sidewalk was the one that most impressed my brother-in-law Tom Bailey, who had cruised over there on his Harley Davidson 74 overhead that night (I don't know whether my sister Maxine was riding with him then or not), but the general feeling was that Porky would live hard, die young, and be missed by everybody but especially the women.

The Korean War changed all that. Porky and Antwine and Walter all went; I had a college deferment, nearly volunteered, then found that otosclerosis would have kept me out. Antwine trained as a paratrooper, Walter was in the Inchon landing, Porky was in the lines for some of the heavy stuff in 1950–51, and they all survived without apparent damage. But when I got back from England in 1954 and next heard of Porky it was said that he had changed—had married, his wife was keeping him on a short leash, and he had got religion. When I finally got to see him again, around 1962 or so, he looked the same—well, not slim spring steel but solid cast iron, hair receding but most of his teeth still there—but he was mild, his words even fewer than before, his whiplash poise changed to a courteous silence. I tried asking him about Korea, and he would only say it was rough. I told him I had heard he became a boxer and won some championships while he was in the Army; he said there was one thing the Army had taught him, that no matter how rough you are there's always somebody rougher. So finally I asked him where he was working, and he said, "I'm a preacher now." Yet he did not try to preach to me, so he may well be a very persuasive preacher.

One thing that strikes me, when I call up such memories, is that Buck Creek people who have stayed local, like Porky or my brother Antwine, have also got around quite a lot. War and job-hunting, curiosity and sheer restlessness, have moved them around and across the U.S., into Japan and Korea and back again. When I think what my uncles saw and lived through, what my Osage brothers and sisters and nieces and nephews and Ponca cousins have been through and seen, it amazes me that a small patch of Oklahoma ground has sent its humans around so far and so variably. The London and New York papers—I use the terms generically, because they are all so charmingly parochial—now and then have sent reporters out to explore the few square miles of terra incognita, mostly scrub timber and barren grasslands they believe, between the Hudson River and the Hollywood Hills, and I recall some pieces in the English newspaper *The Guardian* written by a man surprised to find that people in little Kansas towns had moved around the U.S., and (he reported with astonishment) even other countries, pretty extensively. Not that such discoveries change the minds of editors, or of the chattering classes who fail to realize that the famous *Times* of New York, of Los Angeles, of London, *is* much like the Arkansas River, a mile wide and an inch deep, covering only important people, not real ones.

That's unkind. But when I was getting ready to go out to Tucson one January to read poems and talk about medieval manuscripts, my St. Louis phone rang and it was Don Byron, calling from Arizona to say he had seen a notice in the Tucson paper about the reading, and inviting me to get together with them while I was out there. Don and his beautiful blonde sister had gone to Buck Creek School with us around 1940, when they were living over south of Buck Creek on one of their uncle Dave Ware's places for a couple of years before their folks moved away, first to the little town of Bowring north of us in Osage County, then to Michigan, where Don took a degree in geology from the University of Michigan, his sister a degree with a major in English from Michigan State. He went into mining, set up his own company south of Tucson, and prospered; she married a man who got in good and early at IBM and was sent to set up their sales and distribution offices in France, Italy, Germany, and England in the 1960s and after, then they retired to Tucson in the late 1980s. So when I got out there, they all had me to her house, on a mountainside overlooking Tucson, for a marvelous Mexican dinner, and we talked not only of Buck Creek days, Dave Ware's foxhounds and the Osage Wolfhunters' three day and night hunts up in the Osage Hills, but of time in London and Oxford, Paris and Frankfurt and Rome.

This is not a country whose citizens stay put, and much of the vital energy in its major cities flows from country people who have moved there. But there's another secret that has been kept from the media mutts and money-mongers: in a small town way out there like Pawhuska now, or even along the road through Buck Creek, you may be passing lawyers flying in and out of Washington, D.C., women who have picnicked on the Lake Isle of Innisfree, men who've worked in the Alaskan or Arabian oil fields, soldiered in Saigon, pubbed in London, swamped grapes in California camps, taken doctorates from Heidelberg or law degrees from Harvard, made movies for Ted and Jane. The roads and ditches in Reservation Country have brought in some beads whose value may be dubious, but which do look pretty on the Prestige Exchange, where quite a few citizens of the American Cosmopolis or Pandemonium are now Osage or Ponca, Otoe or Pawnee, Delaware, Sac and Fox, Pottawatomie, Creek and Cherokee and Choctaw and Chickasaw and Seminole, Yuchi and Comanche, Kiowa and Wichita and Caddo, Cheyenne and Arapaho. If Hannibal's Huck and Tom were to light out for the Territory now, they might do well to knock first in Osage country, if only to find a good Interpreter.

Going to College

When I was not yet eleven years old, my white grandfather came looking for me one day. I liked to be off to myself, and one place I could go and not be found was up in the top floor of our garage, which was full of old newspapers, and broken furniture, and cobwebs. The windows were broken and a sheet of tin was nailed over the one to the east. But there was an old rocking chair with one rocker cracked and the stuffing exposed, and I could go up there and sit and do anything, or nothing, on a Saturday or Sunday, and that is where he came looking and found me. He knew something I had suspected but had never let myself think seriously about: he was going to die shortly. He had severe angina, and for the last several weeks when I would go out before daylight with him to milk the cows, he had had to stop, along the path through the weeds of the garden, and set down the buckets and try to catch his breath. So I would wait, saying nothing, because I saw this was a new kind of expression on this whiskery face. He was seventy-two years old and did not want to admit this was not just being a little short of breath, not just the "lumbago" or pain of an old injury from the times of logging, or cutting railroad ties, or hauling the bricks to help build that Triangle Building in Pawhuska, or the hospital where I was born. Even in the dim light from the lantern I held, I saw how serious this was. He did not say anything, just put a hand over his heart and stood for a few minutes. Then he picked up the bucket and started walking fiercely, faster than before—not a man to cower, if he was being called for. When we got to the barn he set the bucket down again at the door, and before unlatching it gasped for a few breaths.

"Well, I don't know," he said, "what's to become of us." I remember it was a cold late February or early March morning—it must have been near his seventy-second birthday, the last day of February, and not long before my eleventh, in March. I see, these many years later, that he was in despair, and I understand that it was not just for himself. What's going to become of us, he said, not of me. We were almost starving. There were seven of us children, my youngest brother not yet a year old, and in those days an Osage headright was worth maybe five dollars a week. My Osage stepfather worked when he could, but a lot of my remembrances from those times involve how my mother had to go in and talk the owner of Landers' Groceries (they were locally owned and named in those days, and I remember Mr. Landers as a very decent man) into taking a check he knew would bounce—and how later she would have to deposit the Osage Payment check and try to make it cover about twice what it was worth in grocery bills and gas bills and cow-feed bills. And in the wintertime there just was not any of the work that put food on the table in summer or fall—no corn to hoe, no hay to pitch or haul, no wheat to shock or shovel. I remember, from those summers, how powerfully my stepfather, Addison Jump, pitched that prairie hay for Mort Murray. I remember too his getting up before sunrise to walk over to Sand Creek, a mile and a half, to hoe corn for Old Man Tayrien, and I recall walking once to do some of that work with him, and looking down one of those half-mile straight rows of waist-high corn on that July day, as we took our lunch break under an elm with the temperature a hundred in the shade, and realizing there was still eighty acres left to hoe—a quarter mile wide, a half mile long. At times like that, even when the alternatives are work or starve, the options are considered. Then as now, hard work was not enough to feed a big family, not even fourteen hours a day of it.

So what my grandfather saw was a family that could not make ends meet. We had plenty of other things to worry about, though, for anyone whose heart was hurting on a cold morning. The house was in lousy shape, and Grandpa saw it would get worse. He knew, as an old hand at helping put up buildings—as I mentioned, he had helped build the old hospital in Pawhuska where we kids were born, the one that stood over on Lynn Avenue not far past the high school—that our house's concrete foundations were crumbling, the front porch sagging and the living room shaky with it, the plumbing gone and the well no longer drinkable. He knew what the troubles with beer and whiskey would be, because he had those troubles himself at times. I won't bore you with all the things you will understand if you yourself have lived among them or now live with them, but I will say this: when I now think of what my grandfather saw, that frosty morning when the eastern sky was so beautiful toward Bartlesville, while I watched bare hills to the east shine as the sun's first diamond-tip broke through the horizon, I know what he meant when he said he didn't know what would become of us.

But when he came looking for me later up in the garage, and I heard his footsteps coming slowly up the stairs to my hideout, I thought he wanted me for some chore. I thought he might want me to help fix once again the gate to the barn-lot, where the great white-oak post he had set there never seemed quite able to hold the rusty iron gate, and it got harder and harder to loop the chain over its nail.

That was not what he wanted. He looked at me where I was sitting, and he saw I was annoyed that my privacy was intruded on. He raised his eyebrows and pursed his lips, the way he usually did when he found himself in the wrong and was being apologetic.

"You reading again?" he asked me.

"No!" I said, "I'm just trying to get someplace I can think a little to myself!" I said it to show I wanted him to leave.

"Well," he said. He looked off to the side. But then he brought his eyes back and looked right at me.

"Mikey," he said, "you ought to go to college."

"Oh," I said. Nobody had said anything about this to me that I recalled. I'd guess, now, that my mother had been talking with him and they had agreed he would talk to me. I was doing well in the school where I was then in the sixth grade—Buck Creek Rural District 66, a mile east of our house on U.S. 60, a fifteen- or twenty-minute walk. My twin sister Maxine and I would usually make A and B grades there. When the state tests were given each year I would score high. It turned out, although I did not know it then, that I was among the highest scorers in Osage County, and when I graduated from the eighth grade in that one-room school, two years later, I was co-valedictorian of Osage County (which was the Osage Reservation), along with Dicky Dickson of Indian Camp School in Pawhuska—two mixed-breed kids at the top, and I think the salutatorian was Patricia James, who used to be with us at Buck Creek but had transferred to Bowring School, a veritable metropolis with maybe a hundred people or more up in the woods-and-prairie ranch country to the north. But when my grandfather spoke to me in the garage there, though I knew he was glad my report cards were good when they came home and my mother signed them, he had never said anything to me about it. So it was clear that he had been thinking in ways I did not know about.

"Go to college?" I said.

"You ought to go to college, Mikey," he said.

Grandpa had not gone to college. He had not gone to high school. He had gone only to the third or maybe into the fourth grade, and then quit and worked in the fields and woods in Missouri where he grew up, in the little town of Doniphan on the Current River by the Arkansas border. When I had learned to read at the age of five in Buck Creek School, with my cousin Roy Camp tutoring me at home, it did not take me long to be reading as fast as Grandpa could read. And in the third or fourth grade, I remember how I was amazed to watch Grandpa sitting in the chair in front of the log fire in our living room and slowly spelling out the newspaper. He had to buy glasses in the dime store, and he could hardly find the ones that would work for him. Only when he was nearly seventy did the first payments of the new Social Security begin that Roosevelt had got put through—I remember Grandpa was paid about seventeen and a half dollars a month at the beginning—and one thing he did was to take some of this money to get reading glasses. Most of it went to put food on our table.

So for Grandpa to say I should go to college was full of meaning to me. And of course I listened, because even though I was annoyed at having my private thoughts interrupted I could see he was serious. And he had helped raise me from a baby, too. I never knew him to lie, and I knew him to be as fair and just a man as there was. I knew he had worked all his life, and I knew he was here with no money and in poor health, and he was working every day to keep this place livable. I remembered how one day I had picked up the newspaper he had been reading about the start of World War II—he always read aloud, slowly and sounding out the words fully as if it was a spelling bee—and I read something aloud, with considerable fluency and ease. He had looked at me oddly, saying nothing, but I was feeling smart-alecky and was showing off, and I just took it that he was a little miffed at me.

"Maybe I ought to go to college," I said to him.

"You ought to go," he said.

He did not say why I should. Nor would he have had any idea how, or where, or with what sort of aims or goals, I was to do this. None of us had gone to college: my mother, and my Uncle Woody, had graduated from high school, but that was about when the Depression hit. (My stepfather had gone to Missouri Military Academy, but that was as far as he wanted to get, and from some of the stories he tells it was maybe farther!) The only one in our family that had got into college was my fullblood Osage uncle, Kenneth Jump, who had got to Notre Dame for a short while before Pearl Harbor, but was taken into the Army after that. Some of the books he had from that little time at Notre Dame were around our house, and one of these—a physics text—would be the thing that got me a scholarship to Tulsa University. But that's ahead of the story.

My grandfather did not say any more to me that day in the garage. He just stood there and looked at me for a minute or so. Then he turned around and walked down the stairs again. Probably one reason I remember the scene with such detail and clarity, more than fifty years later, is that he died on March 28, 1942, not three weeks later, and of course I understood more fully then why he had gone to the trouble of hunting me down that day and saying the few words he said. Just three days before he died he had got up early, on the birthday of my twin sister and me, and put together the makings of a birthday cake: my mother was down with a flu that day, and he did it in place of her. The cake fell, and its two layers—I remember there were two, and I think he said it was a cake for twins and that was why he made two layers—the two layers were very heavy, and very sweet as if soaked in honey, probably because he had used white Karo syrup, sugar being already rationed because of the war. But it was a delicious cake and I am as glad of it as of his telling me to go to college.

Because I did promise him I would go. They would have had to kill me to stop me. I never went on about it, and I made considerable noise protesting from time to time when various people would tell me I should be ambitious, and I ought to use what brains I had, and all that. I usually acted sullen and negative so far as a chance was offered to be sullen and negative. Or so I recall. It got pretty bothersome having people plan my life, and tell me I had this or that or the other ability. Teenagers do NOT like to have other people pushing them to do ANYthing, whether good for them or not. So I did not speak sweetly to my folks, or to people at the high school in Bartlesville who would make noises about college.

But I was going to go. Grandpa had said I should, and I had told him I would.

On the other hand, as I've said, none of us knew how to get into college, or what colleges to look at. And I am a very poor model for anybody who wants to know what the right way to do ANYthing might be. I survived the nickel-and-dime wars that poor people have to fight—people that never have enough to eat, no money to get good clothes or even sometimes enough clothes—but I still fight shame's guerrillas in the back countries of consciousness: worse than not having money is the feeling that you are not so good as the people who look down on you. It was lucky that I had a twin sister to go to school with me, because I can imagine not having been able to stand the hit of going alone from a one-room, eight-grade Buck Creek School, with its thirteen students, to the twelve-hundred-student Central High in Bartlesville. I can easily think how alone I would have been, how slow to find friends, particularly how hard it would have been to learn where other people fitted into the social ranks there in Bartlesville, something my sister Maxine could always tell me. It wasn't books that were tough; I looked at a book the way Babe Ruth looked at a baseball. Where other boys had to fight both books and social problems, I had only the social problems. The hardest need is for some kind of companionship, people you can trust who will respect and trust you as well. People matter so much more than books, and yet the books are what set your status with teachers.

There is always pain, the way I recall it, so much that it is tempting to back away. High school seems in remembering to have been full of miserable moments. I think it is like that for a majority of people, and I think only a few have pleasant and successful high school careers. The high schools I went to were good ones, I see that now. The teachers were more than competent, they really wanted to teach and they were glad to talk with the students. It was the usual situation with the students in the classrooms—boiling hormones and fried brains, under powerful pressure to show up the teachers as stupid and the books as useless and the students as public slaves but private heroes. We were supposed to have this double standard, on the one hand respecting the teachers, on the other despising the stuff they were teaching. Moreover, we *had* to regard the teachers as misguided zealots, tolerated only because they had power to run bad things on us if resisted openly. Same sort of split view of ourselves: students who really seemed to learn the stuff were supposed to be "brains" and held in awe, yet they were nerds for sure and jerks if they took the stuff seriously. To be a pretty girl, a handsome and muscled guy, an athlete and above all to have a car, a motorcycle, a leather jacket of a certain kind, a sweater and skirt and shoes of a certain kind—*that* was what mattered really. Clichés jostled the hallways, jammed the classes.

And only a few of us were rich enough or smart enough—preferably both, since those adjectives were handcuffed together—to go to college. There were plenty of dropouts, a fair number of flunkouts, and not much talk (among ourselves at least) about the reasons for any of this—nothing about dysfunctional families, drug or alcohol problems. Well, I remember hearing that one student was both a drunk and a doper, and he was one of those who vanished from the

school's display-screen when I was in tenth grade, reappeared for a
month or two, and then was gone for good. His family, I think, had
plenty of money, which may have been his problem. And I knew
there were others in the same sort of trouble, if less extreme, because some were friends and many were acquaintances, so I could
see first hand, or hear from those who knew, who had been drunk
that weekend, or worse, that weeknight.

Probably the teachers talked a lot about this sort of thing. I know
some of the teachers would have been up on the family and details for just about every student: Miss Mary Paxton, one of the
best teachers I ever saw, was my English teacher in senior year,
and years later I found she did know a lot about the family miseries and troubles related to classroom problems for most of the
students. I found this out only after she had retired and was living
up in Clarksville, Missouri, her old home town on the Mississippi
a couple of hours north of St. Louis where I was teaching. She had
taught in Bartlesville since the 1920s, and she had driven alone
across America in the 1920s and 1930s when a lot of the roads were
dirt with mudholes and ruts that would stop most lumberjacks. She
had tried to bring black friends to eat in Bartlesville restaurants
when segregation prevailed. She did not have to come to your house
and nose around like a social worker to know what was wrong, what
the troubles and the miseries were. She had imagination, and she
had brains, and she had tough-minded compassion. She knew her
students. I remember being amazed, years later, when I got a letter
from her home in Clarksville saying she had heard one of the radio
talk shows I was on from KMOX in St. Louis with Jack Buck or Bob
Hardy or Jim White, and she corrected my grammar on some point
or other. So I drove up to explain why I goofed like that, and got to
visit with Miss Paxton quite a few times before she died. We sat in
her living room on the bluffs overlooking the great rolling river and
had a lot of talk about the world, and Osage County, and Bartlesville
College High and its students and teachers. I learned more about
my classmates in those talks than I did when I was a student there.

Once, too, she rode back down to Bartlesville with me when I
went to visit folks, and it was remarkable how much she had to say

about current events, and history, and how things got to be this way
in America, and all the things you'd like to think teachers bear in
mind when they are alive, alert, possessed of good minds and beautiful hearts, tough of spirit and shrewd of judgment.

And I had a chance, partly through her, to visit too with some of
my other teachers there—John Haley, for instance, who had taught
American history and was also vice principal and as such had had
to discipline me when I filled out a questionnaire that asked us to
describe what our ambitions were and our plans for the years after
graduation. I wrote on the questionnaire: "What the hell are you
asking me this stuff for? It's none of your damned business what I
plan to do or what my ambitions might be!" or something like that.
Next thing I knew there was this note to come to the vice principal's office and explain my comments to Mr. Haley. Now I thought
of him as a really nice guy, because the year before in his American history class I hit the top on his tests and he had treated me as
a good student, refreshing since some teachers in ninth and tenth
grades seemed to have old favorites and did not want any country
boy coming in and knowing things that only rich kids with nice
folks should know.

But on the subject of that questionnaire Mr. Haley was anything
but a nice guy. I was surprised how stern, and unyielding, he was. It
is of course what "firm but courteous" ought to mean, the way he
dealt with me, but I was just surprised because he had always been
so cheerful and helpful and generous it had made me think I could
say anything. In his history class he had mentioned that he was just
back from Europe (this was 1946) where as a captain in the Army
he had helped liberate France, and I was impressed with the humor
and irreverence of his stories about liberating some cases of canned
fruit for his soldiers, so I thought well, this is somebody that you
don't have to be a stuffed shirt with.

In the vice principal's office, though, it was Captain Haley I was
looking at, and I was up against a near court martial for sacrilege on
his questionnaire. So I explained austerely that I did not like people
prying into my life, and he pointed out that for the first time the
high school people were trying to identify potential college students

and offer them help and advice. I did not tell him that a sore point for me was that offers of help made me feel looked down on. I had done yard work the past summer for a wealthy neighbor of ours, and this neighbor and his wife were among the nicest people in the Buck Creek Valley—yet I resented powerfully what was going on once I figured out that this job was being given as a way of helping me and the family. It was stupid of me, treating pride as principle. When the neighbor's wife made me a most elegant and delicious sandwich for lunch, tuna fish with everything on white special bread neatly quartered and a tall glass of store-bought milk, and her husband said to me in his direct and honest way, "I understand you might be interested in going to college. You know, I could help you," I said to him, "I don't want help—I'll go on my own." Every penny I was making and trying to save up was going to put food on our family table. (Well, I admit this did not include the money spent on going to the skating rink, or buying cherry Cokes at the drugstore for a girl from the rink, or hamburgers after midnight before hitchhiking the eight or ten miles back home from a Saturday night's debauchery with rented skates and Cokes or even malts with the hamburger. I just had no knack for saving, and a lot of excuses for spending. Money did not burn a hole in my pockets, it just found its way into the cash registers before I could stop it.)

So I did not say to Mr. Haley, "Yes, I damn well am going to college, for no reason I understand but because I was asked to go by someone before he died, and I said I would do it." Instead I said Yes Sir, and No Sir, and I Apologize Sir. I said I was not sure what I wanted to make of my life, and when Mr. Haley asked what sort of work I thought I would like to do, I said civil engineering—because I liked trigonometry and I could see that roads and dams and bridges were useful and there was always likely to be the need of building or replacing them. He looked surprised and skeptical, as well he might, since that was the first time I had thought of such a thing, and he likely saw this had bounced straight from the top of my head off the tip of my tongue.

But luckily for me there were to be answers to the hardest question, which he did NOT ask: how in the world could I afford to go to college? At that time, it's true, college was relatively cheap, because teachers were paid even less than now, and costs did not include huge numbers of deans, provosts, lawyers, grant-writers, speech-writers, computer labs, photocopiers and lobbyists and parking lots and quark-ropers and chairs for extinct advisors on foreign policy or authors of failed wars in the Far East, Middle East, South America, Central America, South Dakota, and all that sort of thing. There were very few junior colleges, and graduate programs were small and informal and cheap—at least in Oklahoma—and the money for Veterans Education was still subsidizing the rest of the students. There seemed to be a lot of small colleges around that might have pleasant programs and probably would let you educate yourself fairly well in cooperation with the teachers there.

But in the fall of my senior year I had no idea where I might look to go to college, no idea what I might want to study if I got there, and above all no notion of what I might use for money to transport me there, feed and clothe and lodge me and pay tuition and books and stuff. Clearly enough no help whatever could come from any-one in our family—in our house the cockroaches were about ready to go elsewhere for better meals, and our Jersey cow had died, the chickens were gone and the chicken-house torn down and burned for firewood last winter. This was not a money tree to shake for tu-ition or anything. And this is when my twin sister actually did what had to be done.

A *Going to College* scholarship program had been started up by some imaginative people at the University of Tulsa, to help com-pete with the University of Oklahoma for bright students. O.U. had a wider range of departments, a relatively deep graduate school, and lower tuition than Tulsa University—which was private, small, and teetering near bankruptcy now and then, kept afloat at that moment (as I later learned) by the influx of veterans from World War II. Ben Henneke, a T.U. speech instructor, ran the *Going to College* pro-gram, which was a traveling radio quiz show for high school seniors. Each week Henneke took a small crew around to a different high school, where the top ten or so students would compete and a win-ner would be chosen. Twenty-four winners would be pitted against each other in the semifinals (held in Tulsa at the University), and then for the final show the twelve survivors would come to Tulsa University in late April or May, and the grand winner there would earn a four-year full-tuition scholarship, second place would get two years' tuition, and third place a year's tuition.

There was also a Pepsi-Cola Scholarship Program, this one basing its awards on the SAT scores of selected competitors—the top two scorers in the state would get four-year scholarships to the college of their choice. But the trick to both the Pepsi and the T.U. competitions was getting chosen to compete. I had made pretty good grades, mostly A's and B's with a few C's, but there were a lot of students with better grades and I was just one of the kids who did well in English and fairly well in math and really well in chemistry and history—but not too well compared with some of the students who were acing everything. And the selection for Pepsi and T.U. competitions was actually left up to a student vote, or that was a big part of it at least. (I feel sure, now, that teachers had a larger voice than was officially stated—and it appeared later that Miss Paxton, and Miss Corbin, and Mr. Haley and my charming Spanish teacher Señorita Newkirk—who taught us to sing "La Cucaracha" including some words that would never get by now, *La cucaracha, la cucaracha, ya no puede caminar, porque no tiene, porque le falta, marijuana que fumar!*—had mentioned me as a possible competitor, according to Miss Paxton.) And this was where my twin sister turned the tide: she nominated me, she got all her friends to vote for me, and she had a LOT of friends.

I did not get involved in all that. To tell the truth I thought I could do well on that quiz show; I might be considered bashful but microphones did not scare me. I knew there were smarter students in some of my courses—Johnny Freiburger and Charlotte Carpenter and Benny Williams and Newell Clandy and Jimmy Huff and others—and plenty with better credentials and better work habits. There was David Kindig, who if he had been half as smart as he thought he was would have graduated from Harvard after a semester or two if stupid teachers didn't slow him down. And most of these people I not only liked but suspected could out-test me. My sister, though, thought I was smarter. Looking back, I wish I had got her to take the test; women were kept down, and I was part of that, as I now see. She had once out-spelled me in an English class, and she made straight A's in her Latin courses, and had I been as unselfish as she was I might have managed to get her into some of those college things. It never occurred to me because she had never showed any interest in going to college; she took the typing and shorthand courses and worked in shops and stores while I worked in fields and kennels; and of course Grandpa had not spoken to her but to me, and it's too late now. She had a boyfriend she wanted to marry, and did marry, a good guy, and her story went another way; she was felled by cancer at thirty-three, leaving her two sons, my nephews Jimmie and Tommy Bailey.

So she got me chosen to take the Pepsi test, and that eventually got me placed tenth in Oklahoma on their final exam, and she also got me picked as one of twelve or so Central High students on the *Going to College* quiz show when it came to our auditorium. When I won this it must have surprised a lot of the students, and it was very pleasant to be up there on the stage applauded for winning it, and amazing how long the applause seemed to last. But that only meant I was one of twenty-four students ready for the semi-finals, which would be held in mid-April on the T.U. campus. Meantime, there was the other scholarship to try for on that Pepsi exam—which also would be given in Tulsa, but at Tulsa Central High School.

In those days, Tulsa was a lot farther away from Buck Creek than it is today. Our universe may be expanding, but our home country is shrinking fast. Tulsa was also at that time—contrary to what official statistics would assert—a great deal bigger and more intimidating than now. I had actually traveled as far as Abilene, Kansas, for the National Greyhound Coursing Trials, and having once been to Joplin, Missouri, an enormous maze of very tall buildings, I had even seen big cities—but I had never been to the metropolis of Tulsa before that year. I was sixteen but could not drive a car, so when I had to get to Tulsa for the Pepsi exam in late January, my older brother Antwine drove me down there. It blizzarded that day, snow mixed with sleet driven by high winds, and we had to leave about

5:30 A.M. in the darkness, because I was supposed to be at Tulsa Central High for the exam before 8, and that meant sixty miles in a storm which already had iced the highways and now was dumping ten inches of swirling and drifting snow and ice on top of them.

Only my brother Antwine and his friends could have navigated that storm. We saw cars, trucks, busses that had slid off the road, we saw others slewing and slipping into the ditches, we slid off once ourselves onto the shoulder and stopped with the front end tilted out over a steep embankment, which we would never have got back up if the car had once gone over. I got in front to push, and so did Antwine, and one of his friends put the car in gear and gunned it as we started to push. Trouble was, the guy had put it into second gear instead of reverse, and he nearly ran over us. Luckily, he had quick reflexes—not to speak of how quick OURS were! I had bailed out to the bottom of the ditch before the wheels stopped spinning—and he shifted into reverse, so we managed, after five or ten minutes with help from a bunch of other guys whose car was already hopelessly down in the ditch, to get our car back onto the road.

So we got to Tulsa, to Central High—to which Antwine *knew* the way. I am amazed still when I think of his knowing that. He had dropped out of school in the ninth grade, and he had worked since then and was already husband and father. It was because he had done all sorts of things he was not supposed to, taking the car before he had a driver's license, driving off to Tulsa whenever he pleased, that he knew all this. And it's hard to think of anybody else skillful enough to drive through that blizzard and get us there. I am thinking now of his getting up at 4 A.M. on a Saturday, when a lot of the electric and phone lines along the highway were already down with the sleet, and getting out onto that road, and negotiating as the sleet turned to flakes, small gritty ones that packed hard and slick, then big soft ones draping down in curtains and swirls and spreading a powdery fluff that also hardened and hid the ice on bridges; and those fierce crosswinds, headwinds, tailwinds that tried to ditch us or get us onto the wrong side where a big tanker truck or Greyhound was coming at us. So my sister got me chosen, and my brother got me there. That's worth remembering when someone (me for instance) speaks as if it was my individual abilities that got me there.

The Pepsi exam went fairly well. I remember the pipe-smoking nerd, except he was a tall handsome kid with a girlfriend adoring and in awe of him, obviously very rich (Jesus, he had a tie and maybe a jacket on!) and very sure of himself, who was one of the other exam-takers. But which of those kids was Reford Bond the Third, who turned out to be one of the two winners, I never knew, though I have badminded him ever since. I think that if I had had practice taking this sort of multiple-choice exam (excuses, excuses!) and maybe not marked the whole first page and a half wrong and had to go back and erase and re-mark it, I might have been one of the two winners instead of a tenth-place finisher out of the thirty or so people in the room. Still, I got fifty dollars out of it that paid for a month's rent and food at Tulsa U. eventually—and Reford the Third got a full tuition four years at some posh place, Princeton or Harvard, where his dad Reford the Second and his granddad Reford the First and maybe his great-grandfather Reford the Conqueror had strutted before him. Thus, I regret to say, did envy's aqua fortis spread over one more developing soul its crusty green patina.

But that still left the *Going to College* semifinals. Once more Antwine drove me, this now in blossom time, redbuds pink and misty along to the west of U.S. 75 from Bartlesville south to Tulsa, and dogwood white too where the Osage Hills rise from the prairie there, and around the Tulsa University campus the redbuds and dogwood fading and catalpas starting. The semifinals were in the old Kendall Hall auditorium, and I easily won my half, but there was an ominous note. The strongest other contestant, Bill Sheehan, was a science major (he'd be a doctor), and there were physics questions I could not answer because I'd never taken a physics course. On this semifinal Bill never really got to show his stuff because I was quicker with a hand up on the volunteer questions, and the set questions directed to him did not play to his strengths, as it happened. But I had heard physics questions, and I saw a couple of contestants who lost overall but who could answer those questions and beat Bill to them. They wouldn't be there in the finals, and if there were lots of physics questions then, Bill would win unless I could do something.

This was where Uncle Kenneth's short stay at Notre Dame helped me. When he had gone off to World War II, or sometime thereafter, his books were left off at our house. I don't know whether his mother Grandma Josephine or his sister Aunt Arita had brought them over, or how it came about, but there they were. And my mother had said to me several times (maybe because she knew that while I would wait in the city library for her to come get us after school, I liked to read the science texts including things on radioactivity: in Chemistry we were taught that atoms were made up of negative electrons orbiting positive protons and neutral neutrons, and I had been greatly puzzled how the positives came to stick together instead of repelling each other, and the negatives all whirled around without jumping down into the positives, and I wanted to see what this had to do with the atomic bomb and all, and our chemistry course never got into this)—she had said to me, Well, Mike, you know if you want to look at them maybe Kenneth's books would be useful to you.

One of his books was a physics text. So I sat down, in the week between the semifinal and the final radio quiz show, and learned all the physics I could. On the semifinals there had been questions about light, and the equations by which light intensity on a surface varied with the distance of light source from target surface. I said to myself, I'll be damned if they slide one of those questions by me. I found the parts of the textbook that discussed this, I learned the equations, I did a few of the exercises in the text to see how to answer questions on this. I must have been quick and retentive enough to get away with it then—today I don't remember anything I learned, but remember learning it.

Something, however, got in the way before I could try out this half-baked understanding. Antwine was not going to be able to drive me down for the final, because his boss wouldn't let him off for that day—he was working in a filling station owned by a family that were old friends of ours and another guy had quit and they were short. So my mother was going to have to drive me. She had never had a wreck in her life, but she had one just as we were leaving Bartlesville and pulling out onto Highway 75. We were about to pass a filling station when a high school classmate, Jack Cordell, driving a hot rod he had rigged up, pulled out in front of us. His car semi-stalled, then surged ahead, just when my mother thought she was invited to pass, and we smashed our left front fender into his right. When we got ourselves scraped off the dashboard and untangled the cars, our fender and wheel were so damaged the car was undrivable. The *Going to College* show would start in a little over two hours, and Tulsa was nearly an hour and a half away.

My mother called the filling station where Antwine worked, and cut a deal. Antwine couldn't leave work, but the manager's brother would come by and drive me to Tulsa himself. We waited. We waited twenty-four hours I thought, but it was probably only (as the clocks showed) thirty minutes or so. Then the brother did show up and was very nice—he had had to get his act together and drive over here on no notice, after all—and I got in, and he put the pedal to the metal. My knee was beat up and there were bruises and swelling around my left eye from the fender-bender, but nobody else was hurt and my brain was clear enough. Gene was interested to hear that I was trying for a scholarship; he had gone to Buck Creek ahead of me, and finished eighth grade before going to work. He drove fast. Twenty miles north of Tulsa, POW! the right rear tire blew out, but Gene fought the little black Ford to a standstill without running into the ditch. It took him almost twenty minutes to get the spare on. Still, we got to the T.U. campus just as the Kendall Hall bell rang the hour when the show would start, and I ran up the steps and into its auditorium.

Nobody was there.

In the next five minutes I looked all through an empty Kendall Hall and its classrooms. Nothing. Nobody.

When I came out and stood on its high steps and looked around, I saw down by the U-drive a lot of cars parked in front of another building. It was a Saturday and the campus was very quiet, all in bloom, all green and dreamy, perfectly beautiful and just where I wanted to "go to college."

"Gene, maybe it's over there," I said, and ran down the steps and a hundred and some yards full tilt to Tyrrell Hall, and as I dashed along the sidewalk under its Gothic windows, open to the warm day, I heard voices inside, and I knew it was already going on and I had missed fifteen minutes of the finals. There was a big door to the building: I yanked it open and ran in. The room where the show was being held was on my left, and its door was open, and I saw Ben Henneke facing me with students on his left, and a whole room full of people in between, seated in pews on either side of the aisle. I saw that Henneke was asking a question, and just as his eyes turned toward me running through the door I raised my hand to show I knew the answer, even though I had not heard the question. It sounds like a Ronald Reagan story, but I was thinking: this one's for Grandpa.

Henneke started smiling; his face just lit up. That man was a superb MC—he could have followed Jack Paar as host and Johnny Carson would never have got his chance. I say this with full awareness that Carson is an authentic genius, the best we have seen. And of course that was a small-time radio show there in Tyrrell Hall— but Ben Henneke had bigtime wit, intelligence, charm, aplomb, and a brilliant sense of timing, and so this off-center kid from Buck Creek did not throw that timing off in the least.

"And here is Carter Revard from Bartlesville," he said. "He's missed the first third of the program, and now he has his hand up first for this question."

"Would you repeat the question?" I said. And when he did, I knew the answer, and although it was not exactly by the rules, I think it was fair enough that he gave me the chance to answer it. Besides, as he told me forty years later, all of his *Going to College* crew had private bets (no money, just a cup of coffee or whatever) on who would win the whole thing, and he had picked me, so he had got pretty disgusted when I did not show up at the start of the show.

So how did the contest come out? I was too far behind to win the whole thing, but I did take a third place out of the twelve (which got me a year's tuition scholarship), and I did answer more than one physics question—including one that required me to use the equations from Uncle Kenneth's textbook. And once I got INTO college, people liked my work well enough that they helped me get all the way through it, for better or worse. Wonder what I'd have done, particularly by way of writing, had I gone as laborer or got into the Army just before Korea, assuming I would have survived?

I made choices, or thought I did, but I hardly chose such body and mind as got wrapped around me, or to have had the sisters and brothers, mother and stepfather, uncles and aunts and grandmother and grandfather, who set me on this path and walk beside me. Odd or even, chosen or given, grandpa, we've made it this far.

Report to the Nation

Repossessing Europe

It may be impossible to civilize the Europeans. When I claimed England for the Osage Nation, last month, some of the English chiefs objected. They said the Thames is not the Thames until it's past Oxford: above Oxford, it is two streams, the Isis and the Cherwell. Forked tongue, forked river I suppose. So even though I'd taken a Thames Excursion boat and on the way formally proclaimed from the deck, with several Germans and some Japanese tourists for witnesses, that all the land this river drained was ours, these Oxford chiefs maintained our title was not good, except below their Folly Bridge at most. At least that leaves us Windsor Palace and some other useful properties, and we can deal with the legal hitches later. Also, just in case, I accepted a sheepskin from Oxford with B.A. written on it, and I didn't bother haggling. It will prove I was there; next time if we bring whiskey we can bribe the Oxford chiefs— bourbon only.

So I said the hell with England for this trip and went to France and rented a little Renault in Paris and drove down past the chateaux to Biarritz, stopping only to proclaim that everything the Loire and Seine flowed past was ours. I did this from the filling stations, and I kept the sales-slips for evidence. Oh yes, I waved an arm as I was passing over the Garonne, in Bordeaux, so we now have the area of Aquitaine as I understand the rules of taking possession. The

people there talk differently from those in London, but their signs
are much the same—they use a lingua franca so to speak—so they
recognized my VISA card and gave the Renault gasoline much like
that in Oklahoma, globalized enough so they're not completely be-
nighted. Whether they understood that France now belongs to us was
not clear, but they were friendly and they fed me well, accepting in
return some pieces of beautifully painted paper and metal discs with
allegorical figures on them, with which they seemed almost child-
ishly pleased—if they are this credulous we should not have trouble
bargaining with them when we come to take the rest of France. It
was so easy that I headed on down to Spain.

There, however, some trouble occurred. Everything was crowded
because some ceremony that they hold, the first full moon after
the spring equinox as I understood it (their shamans appear to differ over this and I believe millions of people have been killed dis-
puting it), had filled their marketplaces and the trails and all their
homes away from home—*todas completas*, as the Spanish desk-
clerks everywhere kept saying. So it was back to France, the Spanish
border-guards restamped our papers, no hassles even though I heard
there'd been some bombings, as there had been (I forgot to mention)
in England. The Europeans kill each other pretty casually, by natural instinct it seems, not caring whether they blow up women, kids
or horses, and next day display the mutilated corpses on front pages
or television screens. I mention this so that when we send more
expeditions over the people will take care and not assume everything is as friendly and peaceful as the Europeans would like us to
think. They can surely be treacherous to us if they treat each other
in this way.

After we'd doublecrossed the Spanish border, I thought maybe
we'd slip back up a mountain pass at which the Christians once, or
so their legends say, had headed off some Saracens. Roland's Pass,
they called it, Roncesvalles. Very nice it was, there was a swift clear
stream rushing down the gorge and the road went snaking alongside
and then got higher and higher, single-lane with bulges (like a snake
that had swallowed eggs) for cars to pass each other, till finally we
were way up on the side of the pass looking down two thousand

feet on apple trees in bloom, and shepherds and white dots of sheep down below ignoring us. I waited to claim the country because I realized this was going to be a watershed and if I waited till the top I could get both France and Spain at once. At the top of the pass there was a giant radar station keeping watch on something, evidently not us though. We climbed out of the Renault, looked along the road to where some young men and women were picnicking on a saddle-back, and decided it would be best to climb all the way to the top of a peak to see what we were claiming. From the top we could see way over into Spain and back to France, a lot of mountain gorges with the mist in some of them, real windy but the sky mostly clear with just a cape of clouds blowing away from the Pyrenees peaks to the south of us. We looked down to where the border guards were stopping cars, checking for Saracens no doubt, and then we looked up and there were a pair of golden eagles circling, back and forth over the border guards, and there was a peregrine falcon that crossed fast from Spain into France, none of the birds showing their passports. So I claimed both sides of the Pyrenees for the Osage Nation, but reserved rights of passage for all hawks and eagles, and decided to include said rights also for doves and sparrows—feathers we may want from them once we go to dance there, no use restricting their crossing rights.

Having claimed this, I went on down to see Carcasonne, where we heard the European "spirit of inquiry" had started in the late twelfth century or so and the instruments of torture which helped in these inquiries were still displayed among the heads of Roman statues et-cetera. They had very impressive old walls there, but the wind blow-ing through loopholes and whirling in the empty towers and cham-bers was bitter cold. The ramparts, however, gave us a terrific view over orange-tiled roofs and terraced vineyards to villages (walled) on the hills around, each with its castle, pointing, like football fans chanting "We're Number One." I went ahead and claimed those too, you never know when a ruined castle might come in handy, and some day our kids might want to use one for a Forty-Nine Dance, sort of like Cahokia Mounds across the Mississippi from St. Louis. Then we drove down to Narbonne's beach and dipped our toes in the freezing foaming swells, so we could claim all the shores these

washed. I am a little worried, though, because these waters touch
some lands that we might better sell off to other tribes—water not
fit to drink, all kinds of people mad at each other over things done
two thousand, or one hundred, or one year ago or maybe yesterday
or this morning, all full of land mines and deserts that somebody is
always claiming must be made to bloom or sown with salt again.

On the whole, though, this was a profitable trip. We brought back
several things of local manufacture showing that the people could
be made to clothe and feed us nicely—some dishes, some leather
things. If our elders decide it's worth the bother and expense, possibly we could even teach the poor souls our Osage language, although if our faith and goodness can't be pounded into them we
may have to kill them all. I hope, though, they will learn—although
I concede their history and current attitudes make them look incapable of being civilized. Yet even if they prove intractably savage
they can serve as bad examples to our children. They do not know
how to use the land, for one thing—they insist on spreading oil and
tar all over it. They dry out rocks and reduce them to a powder, transport them hundreds of miles, pour water on it and make it back into
rock, and then build their houses out of this stuff. They cut up cliffs
and use the pieces to imitate aisles of tall forest trees, and they melt
certain rocks and make transparent sheets of it, colored with certain
powdered rocks, to imitate the colors of autumn leaves. This shows
how ingenious they are, and how they misuse their cleverness, since
the stories of their sacred ceremonies that are represented in these
colored sheets could be told in the forests among the autumn leaves
if they chose, saving the trouble of moving all that rock. I must
admit they get some pretty effects this way. It would be nice to have
one of these shrines to look at now and then. They certainly have
a lot of torture scenes in them, and these are the models for their
spiritual life they say. That may explain the bombings that keep
happening among them, and the threats of wiping out their enemies
with so many different kinds of weapons. We could put together a
great museum, if our people wanted, with the skeletons of such vic-
tims, and the religious clothes and such—there are plenty of these
inside the shrines I mentioned, and even though they seem to ob-

ject to having these things dug up, I expect a few drinks of firewater will pacify them, and if not we can pacify them with sharper tools. But of course we might not want to collect such barbarous things— it's just a thought. We should, though, have something to remember them by, in case we have to wipe them out as incapable of rising to our level, and it would be easy to convert one of their shrines into such a museum, the Sainte Chapelle in Paris for instance.

In sum—to conclude this part of my report—we have now got much of England, France, and Spain, and a good claim to all the lands with Mediterranean shores. I see no reason why we should not send as many of our people as want to go, and let them take up residence in any of these places. It would at first be a hard and semi-savage life, and there would be much danger from the Europeans who in many cases would not understand our motives. As a chosen people, we would probably have to suppress some opposition, and at times it might be best to temporize. We will, however, as the su-perior race, triumph in the end.

But hold on a minute: our elders, I realize, don't want to do things the way my report has been suggesting—they think that's too much like the Europeans did our people, and they think we should be more civilized. They do have a point, and we culture-warriors should listen carefully. So I have been wondering—should we even bother with the military side of things? Maybe instead of sending people over to take the land, and drive people off and starve those that won't leave into submission, and show them how to live and wor-ship by force if need be, we'd do better just to transport Europe over to us, and not try to counterpunch Columbus. I have even thought of a way to do this, because I did go on past those late staging areas from which Chris jumped off, and I got back closer to where their power sprang from, first in Rome and then in Greece, and though I did not get to Damascus and Jerusalem and Mecca, or to Peking where what went around is coming around, I saw how we can cram most of Europe into a computer and bring it back to deal with on our own terms, far more efficiently and cheaply than by trying to load all that geography on our backs the way Ameropeans have done. We can turn everything of theirs into electrons dancing around at our fingertips, words or corporations or whatever.

So I've started by looking carefully at Vesuvius and the villas which it saved by destroying, and the fine pornographic walls there, the neat body-casts in volcanic ashes and some of the words left here and there, geo-graphics made out of graffiti. These fitted easily into my preconceptions and cost very little to bring back to Pawhuska, if anybody here should want them. And while we admittedly don't have a volcano handy in Osage country, we do have other things that show us how destroying has been used in theory to save. You may recall my letter in the *Osage Nation News* not long ago, reporting on rock shelters, but in case that's not to hand, here's a copy:

Rock Shelters
(*for John Joseph Mathews*)

Up here, bluff-slabs of sandstone
hang out from the rim,
painted blue-gray with lichens, sheer
over dusty level of a
sheltered place: water sometimes
down over places worn and knobby drips
and darkens, softens earth to hold our
lifeprints; buttercup and rock pink
live where the hickory's branches fight
the sun and wind for power, but mostly here's
just humus: leaf-mulch deep and rustling
between great boulders broken from rimrock sliding
invisibly down the steep slope, The walk
down through these to the creek that
runs some of the year below here,
thin and clear over silty sandstone's
edges and angles, is short, steep, shady. Stoop
back beneath this shelter, we're in dust,
but in this damp earth just outside
the overhang are mussel shells—
worn
to flaky whiteness, rainbow of

iridescence long since dead. Here's charcoal too,
deep under the hanging slab. See,
we were
once here.
Moving with Doe Creek down
to where it joins Buck Creek,
down this narrow shallow canyon choked
with rocks you come out where
the trees loom higher, elm and pinoak columns
rise and arch dark over earth
loamy and loose and the creekbanks
of steep sandy clay, roots jutting over pools
muckbottomed winding down to Buck Creek and
mingling where it moves from
sandy shallows down to springfed depths
and darkness. Here, the winter
surrounded deer and turkeys, here lived plenty
of beaver, muskrat, mink and raccoon, fox and
bobcat and cottontail, coyote slinking, quail
and squirrels, mice and weasels all with
small birds watching from the bush or grapevine, berry
tangles, juncoes, waxwings, cardinals like blood on
snow, all sheltered here from
the prairie blizzards north.
And southward, in the bend of
Buck Creek level to the southern ridge a valley
of bluestem bending thigh-deep under
sunflowers nodding, meadowlarks flying and singing with
grazing buffalo, red wolves and coyotes trotting watching
with pricked ears a hunter crawl with
bow and arrows for a shot.
Now crossed
by asphalt road, wire fences, lanes to white farmhouses
where no farming's done, grapes and lettuce and
bananas on the polished table from Texas, from
California, Nicaragua, the orange-fleshed
watermelons that once lay in sandy fields by
Doe Creek gone, as truckloads of melons rumble
past from Louisiana into town where food is
kept. To plant here, you buy. This land

was needed, we were told—it would be used. So oil
is pulsing from beneath it, floats dead
rainbows on Buck Creek and draws brief trails
straight as a Roman road across the sky, where people sit
drinking and eating quietly the flesh of what
has followed buffaloes to winter in
the valleys underneath, on which
sky-travelers look down.
This new world
was endless, centered everywhere, our study
of place and peoples dangerous, surprising, never
completed. Doe Creek
tasted different from Buck Creek and our people still
did not look all alike.
How far, meant counting
the streams that must be crossed.
The reasons why were everywhere, uncircumscribed—
stars twinkle, moon never does, they both
were relative to whippoorwill and owl.
Greenwich did not
keep time for us. Now, the small stars
move fast and send down messages of war
to speech machines or pictures of
pleasure to our living rooms, inviting us out into
a larger endlessness with many
centers. Galaxies, before long, will
be sold for profit, once the first space-ship has
claimed one and the next has come to
kill all those before. Think
of walking on blue stars like
this one, new
plants, new beings, all the rock
shelters where we'll crouch and see
new valleys from.
Here's my
mussel-shell. Here's the charcoal.
We were here.

As you see, it is simple enough to bring Vesuvius and the Roman
Empire back, and as for what evaporates in transit, it is easier for

our people to go over and enjoy the flavor of it there than send war-dancers over to annex it and have such troubles with the local savages as would be sure to break out. So in case our elders don't want that bother, here's Rome freeze-dried into a poem.

Unfortunately Greece is giving me a little more trouble getting processed. We took a ferry over to Corfu, and then in the town across from Corfu we rented a Volkswagen and drove it across northern Greece, through the Pindus Mountains, to Olympos. We stopped a while in Meteora, to look at that huge rock mountain or tower with all the caves which were lately used by religious hermits. There were great black and white birds sailing in the updrafts around the heights of that place, and I thought they were eagles, but they turned out to be storks. This might explain the guidebook's curious statement about how the medieval hermits became so numerous—they *went into the rocks and multiplied*, it said, and there ARE old Christian legends about storks bringing babies. But what we really wanted to do was drive in the mountains, and I was particularly anxious to get up Mount Olympos, that being the place where Greece's head deity was when Greece was doing things that mattered for a few thousand years. And so I traced the power back up along the Vale of Tempe, under the mountain, and toward its source, since they have a road that lets Volkswagens up clear to the top of Olympos. We got slowed down by a blowout though, and spent the middle part of a sunny chilly spring day beside the green-gray River Peneus, looking up at the great massif of Olympos, and repairing the tire, and eating honey and bread and peanut butter and drinking Coca-Cola. But we found we could drink the spring water around there, showing that the old gods are friendly still, and we filled our empty plastic Coke bottles from Aphrodite's spring, and Apollo's spring, and Dionysus' spring, and the Muses' spring—see, I brought back some in this container, and the water neatly fitted the sides of the cowpond in our bluestem meadow:

To the Muses, in Oklahoma

That Aganippe well was nice, it hit the spot—
sure, this bluestem meadow

is hardly Helicon, we had
to gouge a pond, the mules
dragged a rusty slip scraping
down through dusty topsoil into
dark ooze and muck, grating open
sandstone eggs; but then the thunder
sent living waters down, they filled
the rawness with blue trembling where white
clouds sailed in summer and we
walked upon the water
every winter (truth
is a frozen allomorph of time), though it
was always more fun sliding. We'd go and
chop through six-inch ice by the pond's edge, pry the
ice-slab out onto the pond from its
hole where the dark water welled
up cold to the milk-cows sucking noisily,
snorting their relish; and
when they'd
drunk we shoved the ice-
slab over to where the bank
sloped gently, took
a running chute and leaped atop the slab real
easy and slid,
just glided clear over
the pond riding on ice —
or stretched prone
on the black windowy ice looked
down into darkness where fish dimly
drifted untouchable beneath our fingers.
Ice
makes a whole new surface
within things, keeps
killer whales from seals just long enough to
let new seals be born before they
dive in to feed or be fed upon.
—Come sliding now, and later we'll
go swimming, dive in with the
muskrats, black bass, water moccasins, under

> this willow let the prairie wind
> drink from our bare skin:
> good water
> fits every mouth.

I noticed that shepherds in those Greek mountains were very friendly and I regret missing the chance to cement a relationship when one asked in sign language for a cigarette I didn't have—they have taken up our discovery of tobacco's offering-power, but denuminalized it, which makes it hard on their lungs. This shepherd gave his name as *Aristo-tell-Ace,* and on the whole his mountain seemed worth claiming since its water (unlike that in Rome, which is full of Mussolini's Revenge) the gods and muses still approve; so after changing the blown-out tire we drove from the Vale of Tempe up Mount Olympos. But we did not get all the way to the top, which could be why I have trouble fitting Greece into the word-processor. The blowout cost us quite a bit of sunlight and also reduced the Volkswagen temporarily to four healthy wheels, so we got worried that one of them might be gored by the road, which turned from asphalt to broken stone at about eight thousand feet. Olympos is only something under ten thousand feet but very husky, sprawls a lot with spurs and gorges, and the road keeps winding and zigzagging up one perpendicular ridge and over onto another. It was when we got onto the dirt and rocky road, and from its edge looked down on eagles soaring over several thousand feet of updrafts, and a pine tree had fallen across the road and we had to drive slowly around its tips by the cliff-edge and those on the side next the eagles got nervous, that we decided to claim only as much of Greece as this level of Olympos would allow us to. So we may not have got above the Aonian Mount and this may mean trouble for our epic Osage work at least in English, until the next expedition, but that's for the elders to decide.

What gave me pause when we decided to turn around was the sound of thunder. Since I am of the Thunder people, I wondered whether this was saying to go on up, but then we noticed that some distance out toward the Aegean Sea, on the plains under Olympos, was where the thundering came from, and when I got out of the car and walked over to the rim and listened and looked, it was clear that those were cannons firing, and so I did not believe it was an oracle to go up after all. Later we found that these were army exercises, and tanks firing, near the Greek army's base near Olympos. But at least, in looking for the thunder's source, it was possible to see that the view from Olympos across the Aegean was fine as wine, and the peninsula where Mount Athos is situated was in plain sight over some aquamarine and amethyst distances which darkened to emerald and purple as the light began fading. We dropped back down into the twilight, and joined the tanks going home, and so it would now be possible for any Osages to feel free to use whatever comes down from Olympos, such as epics, tragedies, democracy, either the honey or the honeybees (to misquote Sappho), odes, civil wars of people or gods or both, good water, idealism, all that.

I don't think it is useful to say much more about Greece. Athens we should not bother with; it is too much like Paris and London—everybody tries to be someplace else at the same time, so the paths are all knotted up, covered with asphalt and smog. Like Paris and London and Rome, Athens is full of ruins, but easier to get to than theirs, and on the whole prettier and less cluttered with people living in them. We did go down, also, and had a look at Argos, where Agamemnon took a bath the way Custer took a ride, and then we drove across the Peloponnese to Olympia—by sandy Ladon's lilied banks, the scenic route through Arcadia, where death was the shepherd's friend, and there were redbuds in mauve pink bloom among the fallen marble columns at Olympia—nice to see the Oklahoma state tree there. And there was also a dead European adder, smashed and dried, lying on one of the column-stumps where the lizards were frisking in bright sunlight. I don't know why, in Europe, poison snakes never invented rattles to warn people, but this one evidently did not get in the first strike. On the whole I would be for our claiming all the Peloponnese, including Argos as well as Olympia, because it could be useful to us—what the hell, we might as well have pastoral as well as epic and tragedy if we want to claim Europe for our kids. And it is probably our destiny anyhow, if our elders won't mind such an Ameropean way of putting it, to get the whole subcontinent. I sneaked a piece of the Peloponnese into a lyric as one sample of how it plays on the rez:

As Brer Coyote Said,

the country's not quite
all field or fence, blackberries
root wild on stony soil
among scrub timber, vines
thorny still in winter as booted feet thrash
through hip-high hay, brown and stemmy, after
the dogs and rabbits running blind
to blackberry briars until
they've grabbed and torn, saying
this ground is taken for the smaller nations who
live BENEATH, who perch BETWEEN—
surviving too spring's burning with the wind swinging
its gold-crackling scythe across
the meadow purging
old nests and vines among rock-croppings
as dried cow-chips go smoking
back to the sky or floating
creekwards with rains and leave the
marginal things such black clarity to grow in, wild
plums whiten, chokecherries bloom
along winding gullies,
new shoots spring green and fork
the air like snaketongues coming out
of eggs to flicker tasting—
the vines flower loosely as sunburn
days move in, bare feet
grow tough enough to walk
among thorn fringes on the way
down to the low-water bridge
(the rock-riffles and pool darkshining
under arch of elms like a water-floored
cathedral,
brown naked bodies poise,

                    fly on the ropeswing down from
                        their high bank and skim
                    with one heel to rise up, up,
            and drop through topwater's warmth into brown
            darkness of spring-cold upwellings like waving
                    tendrils around the thighs)—
                            and July,
                        July is BERRIES—
                    the heaping pans and
            handled buckets spilling their black shining
                    with some a tight
                            red still
                and reaching fingers, even stung
                    by a hidden wasp to swell
                like soft cucumbers, are consoled
        by cobblers, whose thick doughs and crusts purple
        with juice and flake with sugar under yellow spilling
        Jersey cream into blackpurple berries that taste
                        like nothing else
                waiting in roadside ditches,
                    rockpiles, woodmargins—
                            FREE
                    between their thorns.

Well, I am going to end this report for now, only adding that I hope
some better fate befalls me than fell on the European conquistadores
—you know how Cortez ended up running alongside the chariot
of Charles the Fifth, crying about never having been given a piece
of the empire he had conquered; and Balboa, Pizarro and the rest
got hanged or assassinated. Anyhow Europe, being secondhand and
pretty badly used, ought not to be priced so high as Louisiana when
Jefferson bought from a French dictator the land on which, as he
knew and did not know, our Osage people happened to exist. Freeze-
dried as in these words, Europe in any event won't be worth things
of serious value. So don't let any of us offer language, traditions,
beadwork, religion or even half the Cowboy and Indian myth, let
alone our selves, this time. These words, whatever has evaporated,

will give its aftertaste, enough for anyone wanting to steal a culture from under the noses of its guardians; they wouldn't let me take the gold mask of Agamemnon, but I did sneak out with his story.

Still, remember that Coyote outsmarted himself and lost his beautiful fur. (Kept his wits though. Wonder how things would have gone if it had been Coyote not Oedipus up against that Sphinx. Europe with a Coyote Complex . . . hey, maybe it WAS Coyote!) Comedy is worth more than tragedy any time where survival is at stake. Always tricky, of course, claiming another continent, especially when you succeed, as I hope we are about to do; and then Sion's hill, and Sinai, though a few hundred years of recycling may be needed first for those. Meantime, keep the oil wells pumping, and let me know if you have any "special" orders for pieces of Russia, China, Japan, or even "India."

Yours ever,
Special Agent Wazhazhe No. 2,230

P.S.—Speaking of Jerusalem, how retroactively can we claim a place? I forgot, in passing through the Dordogne and Spanish areas, to claim the caves at Lascaux and Altamira, etc., but here is a piece of metamorphic rock or maybe a geode that might get them back for us.

Stone Age

Whoever broke a rock first wasn't trying
to look inside it, surely,
just looking for an edge
or meant to hammer something, and it broke.
Then he saw it glitter,
how *bright* inside it was; noticed how things
unseen are fresh. Maybe he said
—it's like the sky, that when the sun has
crashed down through the west
breaks open to the Milky Way, so we see
farther than we are seen for once, as far

as light and time can reach and almost over
the edge of time, its spiral track like agate
swirls in rock from when it still
was water-stains, had not yet found its
non-solution to the puzzle
of dissolution, keeping within its darkness
the traces of its origin as day keeps night and
night keeps stars. Pebbles, headstones, Altamira,
dust-wrinkles over darkness.
What shines within?

Family Reunion

Hadn't seen my youngest brother and his kids for quite some time. You know how it is here in America, we try to get as far as possible from each other. I mean, the main theory of *family* in psychology seems to be that families which stay together are abnormal—if you try to live near your parents you are abused, and plan to murder them. Why else was Oedipus the model for psychoanalysts to explain the Modern Family's usual condition? Besides, the real reason for coming to America, according to the theory of the Melting Pot, is to *forget* who you were in Europe, or Asia, or even Mexico. (The Africans had *their* old selves dissolved away, of course, on the slave boats.) Once you get here, the idea is to be *only* yourself. Naturally this means you have to disperse: if you belong to some ethnic group you had better move away from them and be really American like the rest of us, or them. It's hard for New Yorkers to do this but even they *can* go to California or Florida to lose their old names, classes, histories. There you can start over, and nobody can hold your past against you, you can invent one if needed. You can make your fortune, and if you want to send a little back to your unmelted kin, your *lumpkins*, the thing for them to do with it is move to Florida, where there are no seasons, just as in Los Angeles the leaves never fall, same as in Eden. Well, I'm probably way out of date with that picture, the place to go now may be San Diego or Vermont, or San Antonio or Santa Fe or some other place properly sainted or desert-like.

Which applies sort of to us here in St. Louis, right in the Middle,

where the Mississippi and the Missouri get together not far from the
Ohio, where things float by from the Rockies and Great Lakes and
Appalachians, down to this center of America where a lot of people
for a long time have been gathering and passing on to somewhere
else—future, past, whatever the visas allow. And our family, as I
say, have pretty well followed the American pattern. I mean we're
mixed. I'm Irish, Scotch-Irish, French, Osage Indian, though when
I publish as poet I can be only ONE of the Above. My half brother
Addison, who's half Osage and half Scotch-Irish and Irish I guess,
works for the Defense Department and lives near King George, Virginia, but he married a Lakota woman and their two kids are, well,
all those things together. So Addison and I were born in the Osage
Agency town of Pawhuska (which means White Hair, a name gained
by an eighteenth-century chief who took a white wig from a British
officer in lieu of a scalp) in Oklahoma (which means Land of the Red
Man, a name given to indicate that it was forever Indian Territory),
and four of our brothers and sisters still live back in Oklahoma, but
here I am in St. Louis, and there Addison is in Virginia, and we
have cousins out in California, and others of Ponca and Irish etcet-
era over in White Eagle and Red Rock and Stillwater and all those
Oklahoma places, and God knows where the rest of the Scotch-Irish
and French-Osage branches have got to by now, which rivers flow
beside whatever harps they hang on the willow trees thereby. And
with Addison working now for the Defense Department in Virginia,
and finishing his Ph.D. in mathematics, we rarely get to see him.

So I was happy one summer when he and the kids could get by
here for a visit, on the way back from their brief time with Oklahoma folks. I wanted them to come down and meet some friends
at the American Indian Center of Mid-America, where I serve on
the Board. And they wanted to see the stainless steel Arch here in
St. Louis, and ride up the elevator to its six-hundred-thirty-foot observation windows over the Mississippi, and I wanted to take them
over the river to Cahokia Mounds, where the largest town north of
Mexico had flourished some hundreds of years before Columbus hit
this hemisphere.

We almost forgot to look for the eclipse promised for that day—

but coming out of the American Indian Center of Mid-America, my Osage nephew Aaron, or his sister Kimberly—well, their Lakota mom Grace will give me hell unless I say they are Osage *and Lakota* (and for that matter their Irish and Scotch-Irish grandma is up there reminding me of the Camp and Kelley share in all this, all those gatherings from the Fanad Peninsula just west of Londonderry, and from the Black Hills, and the Big Spring on Current River in the Ozarks, and the sandy windings of Bird Creek and Buck Creek among the Osage encampments, and all the way from Mont Revard in the Savoy Alps)—ah, anyhow either Kim or Aaron said, just as we were about to climb into my little blue Japanese Mazda there on our Center's asphalt parking lot, "Hey, Dad! we forgot the eclipse today!"

"Oh yeah," Addison said, "it must have happened already." He looked sideways at me and said, "While you were introducing us in there to the Seneca Receptionist and the Meti Custodian and the Cherokee Employment Specialist and the Anglo Outreach Worker, and finding out that your Comanche Executive Director had been called out to help a Dogrib lady settle a little matter of a brick through a windshield and a bullet through the hip."

"Well," I said, "we have to make sure these members of the Indian Diaspora get together now and then. Never a dull moment around our Indian Center, unless you're waiting for an eclipse. You think it's over?"

"No, Dad," Kim said, "look how the sunlight is, kind of strange— maybe it's still going on."

"Sure," I said, "the paper claimed it would be visible from after one till three o'clock. It's only two-fifteen. You're right, Kim, the light *is* weird, even with that high haze of clouds and this St. Louis steam-bath humidity."

"I see it!" Aaron said. "Part of the lower edge is dark, see?"

"Don't blind yourself, you guys," Addison said.

"One way we worked it, last time an eclipse came here," I said, "was looking down at the leaf-shadows on the sidewalk. The leaves block most of the light, but where the sun comes through them it's like a point source of light, a pinhole in a *camera obscura*, except it's not just one, it's a whole lot of little glowing spots with one part dark."

Kim and Aaron led the charge, across the lot into the shade of a big sycamore. We looked down at the sidewalk there, but saw only blurry shadows. The leaves were too high, too few. They let too much light through, no pinhole sources.

"We could try my glasses maybe," I said. I took them off and held them so the focal points were on the sidewalk, but all they made was dazzling spots that couldn't quite be seen as showing any dark edge. My brother took his off and tried. They were a little better, not much.

Aaron straightened suddenly and bolted toward the Mazda. "Binoculars!" he yelled back. He had brought them from Virginia, used them on the long drive to Oklahoma and then to St. Louis, spotting the license plates on cars ahead of them, staring at hawks on telephone poles or soaring high over a rest-stop—all the ordinary unsuspecting creatures and things that get interesting if you can bring them close, but not so close they might grab or sting or look back at you.

Aaron grabbed the binoculars, slammed the Mazda's door and came trotting back. I had to say, "Don't try and look at the sun through those, Aaron!"

"Oh no—I'll let the sun come through them to the asphalt and see if that will show the blacked-out part." His father pulled a white handkerchief out and spread it on the sidewalk.

"Great, Dad!" Aaron said.

And there it was: the round unbearably bright spot with a black curving bite missing at the lower left. Not as clear as I remembered the many glowing disks beneath our sweetgum tree, the time of our last eclipse, but we all saw it. Just a little—you had to know what you were looking for, but there it was.

How old Kim and Aaron will be, or whether their dad and I will still be around to try looking at the next eclipse, who knows?

So as the light sharpened again, and the steamy St. Louis heat bore down even harder, we buzzed away from the Indian Center and onto the Interstate, along that to the Poplar Street Bridge across the Mississippi. I wanted to make sure my niece and nephew looked back in time at what we were passing high above.

"We're just downstream from where the Missouri joins the Mississippi," I told them. "That's where the Great Sioux Crossing was, where our great-great-great-grandparents got together to trade. Indian peoples would come down from way up in the Dakotas or Montana along the Missouri, and down from Minnesota or Canada on the Mississippi. They could come down the Illinois River that joins the Mississippi just north of where the Missouri goes in. And they maybe came up from where the Ohio joins the Mississippi not far south of here, and the Ohio comes down from Pennsylvania and West Virginia. So you had people bringing things down here from the Rockies, and the Great Lakes, and the Alleghenies, and for that matter up the Mississippi from Louisiana and the Gulf of Mexico. There was a big Mound Builder civilization centered here, and a string of towns up and down the Mississippi and Ohio and as far west as Oklahoma. Archaeologists dig up things that came north from Mexico, south from Canada, east from Wyoming and Montana and maybe the Pacific, west from the Appalachians and all."

"It doesn't really look too wide here, where we're crossing," Kim said.

"That's true, where we are the Mississippi is hardly wider than the Thames in London, at least when the tide is in," I said. "It's a lot wider just upstream because there are a lot of locks and dams and it looks more impressive, and the bald eagles hang out there in winter because they can catch fish in the open water below the locks and things. Every January there's an Eagles Day and not long ago Lawrence and I drove up there and counted twenty-nine eagles near Clarksville, mostly sitting around in the trees but some of them skimming down and catching fish."

Across in Illinois, we headed east and north on I-55, toward Cahokia Mounds where the great urban center had flourished for many hundred years and died out mysteriously just before Columbus. We followed the Great River Road signs among reedy swales and sloughs with cattails bending where the redwing blackbirds were perching and spreading their wings and fluting. We saw a line of white cattle egrets winging slowly past.

"See those white birds?" I said, not missing a chance to educate the next generation. "All the way from Africa. They flew the Atlantic. Got here on the trade winds like Columbus."

"The whole Atlantic?" Aaron said.

"The whole way. Not so long ago either that they first got to America. They're spreading west and north. They got across the Southeast from Florida, up into Arkansas. Back in the sixties I first saw some in Oklahoma, over by Grand Lake. They stand around and catch insects in the fields around the cattle, that's why they call them cattle egrets I think."

"I wonder how they navigate," Addison said.

"Me too, I even wonder what they have in mind when they take off from Africa, just fly up from some marshy place by the ocean I guess. I can't imagine what they thought they were doing, the ones that first got up into the wind and went out to sea. What in the world would a bird have in mind to just keep going west, with nothing but ocean underneath it? They used to say cattle egrets got over here by perching on ships or something. Anyhow they got here. Even then, why would they keep on moving from Florida to Alabama and Mississippi and up the Mississippi to here? Scientists even yet can't say how homing pigeons find their way back to a place, I guess it's too much to ask them to look into the neural pathways that kept these big old birds sailing westward like Daniel Boone to settle in these parts."

"I see the mounds, Uncle," Kim said.

"That's them," I said. "I used to drive by here and never notice. Now they have signs to tell us how to get off and see them. See over to the left, that's a wood-henge they've reconstructed, those cedar poles set in a big circle there?"

"Was that what the Indian people here made?"

"That's it. The poles are set just where anybody standing at the center can know where to expect the sun, or moon or stars or whatever, at just the right time of the year. That way they knew the right time to start their ceremonies up on the temple mounds or wherever."

"Yeah, Dad," Aaron said. "These were like computers they were using. They'd probably have made you one of their wise old priests."

"I guess you're right," my brother said. "They probably developed math enough."

"I bet they did," I said. "These guys were in close touch with the Aztecs and Mayans. Those Mayans introduced the zero well before Europeans borrowed it from Arabs. Your daddy has probably told you long ago that the word zero is from the Arabic language. Arabic numbers, Arabic zero. These Mound people probably borrowed numbers from the Mayans the same way. They seem to have sacrificed human beings here sometimes. Not too different from when you Computer People in the Defense Department there in Virginia made flowcharts that direct a Tomahawk Missile the safest way to Baghdad."

"I suppose that's true," my brother said. "They probably were just as proud when the eclipses came on time as we all were when the TV people said the missiles we had programmed did exactly what they were supposed to do."

I didn't want to get much further into all that. I work for a university that depends on defense spending for fighter planes and such. So we zipped on over to the Visitors' Center and made a beeline to the cafeteria and had some Cokes and hotdogs, not to mention bratwursts.

"Oh man!" Kim said, "These eclipses really make you dry!"

"Not to mention your Uncle Professor's explanations," my brother said.

So then we walked around the terrific exhibits where caring and clever and careful people have brought alive that old City of the Flood Plain here. Down in the sawdust and woodchip pits the lifelike dummies of men, women, children stand or squat, gazing just to your left whenever you think to look them in the eye. Makes you want to wake them up. There are their houses, here are their beautifully crafted pots and weapons and toys. We went in to the movie's darkness and heard a voice from some famous white person apparently now dead or maybe not—who can say with a voice, nowadays?—that told us how these Unknown People had done their things and passed away. Then we went into the Museum Shop and got some things, and I gave Addison a book for his fiftieth birthday, a book called *Indian Givers* by Jack Weatherford.

I sneaked a look into Weatherford's book before I gave it to him though, while Kim and Aaron were reading some booklets and Addison was looking through the postcards. It starts with the Silver Mountain high in the Andes at Potosi and how its mines and those of Mexico were dug by Indian slaves for the Spanish and financed the beginnings of European capitalism, and then how the beginnings of corporation structure came from the Canadian and the Virginia settling and trading companies, so Indian capital and the innovations that came in as a result of figuring how to set up colonies created the modern corporate and state structures and of course all this paid not only for the enslavement of Indian peoples but also for much of the Great Art of the Renaissance as well as European wars in the next few centuries.

I even started to read about the way the Inca potatoes changed Ireland and Russia (vodka's made from potatoes, it seems) and Poland and Germany and all, and tomatoes in Italian cuisine that came from Peru and so forth, but Addison came over to see what I was up to and I just went ahead and handed him the book and said here, I thought you ought to get educated now that you're a mature individual, and he said well he expected the professor would give him something educational, but thanks anyway it was the thought that counted. I did say it was a fascinating book and he would want to read it right away and all. He was polite about it and properly grateful. It was not till later that month that I got my own copy of Weatherford's book and finally got into the whole business about curare and quinine and all the things we gave to feed and heal people who would do their best before long to starve and poison Indians in the name of Aristotle and Jesus, according to the famous debates between Sepulveda and De Las Casas around 1550 when De Las Casas argued that it was monstrous to do such things, that the Indians might really be human beings. . . .

We climbed the steps (old railway ties?) up to the top of the highest mound at Cahokia. It's called Monk's Mound, after some Trappist Monks who set their retreat up on its top for a while, maybe to exorcise old demons of the New World. Now the monks are gone, and so are the orchards they put there, but the mounds are still solid. From that highest one you can look westward across the Mississippi and see the great stainless steel Gateway Arch, designed by Eero Saarinen and built by a lot of men who never get mentioned, including some of the "Mohawks of High Steel"—Don White, for instance, a big husky Seneca steelworker and crafts trader I see at our pow-wows and elections, and Mike Brooks, an even bigger guy (Seneca too, I think). The Arch looks like part of a Titan's handcuff sticking up where it locks the city into the dream called Forever Westward. It has neat little elevators inside its hollow legs and they go ratcheting up with four or five passengers in molded plastic seats, and when we were sightseeing there we all started to cram into one but just as the door started to close my brother Addison suddenly lunged and scrambled out and turned and said, "You guys go on up, I'll meet you back here when you come down." I hadn't known he was claustrophobic; me, I am more afraid of heights than of closed places.

But we had no trouble whatever hiking up the steep timbered steps of Monk's Mound, and once we were on top and rubbernecking there, an intermittent stream of tourists and hikers, some looking to be retirement age, flowed up and around and past us there, some talking, some quiet, all friendly, giving off happiness. And there were short brunettes in shorts, and tall tanned racers in running shoes panting up the long flights of steps, turning round and stilting down again. And butterflies, drifting in the constant gusting winds up there—three tiger swallowtails, some sulfurs, painted ladies, a fritillary. And when we went down, toward the asphalt parking lot, we took a shortcut over rough greensward, beneath black cherry trees with their tall scaly-barked trunks. There were bittersweet cherries dangling from their stems down to our fingers, or underfoot and squashing in the sweat-lodge heat. Smog blurred the St. Louis buildings across the Mississippi, smeared gray haze in front and around its dark-glassed *Terminator* buildings.

"See over there, there used to be a lot of mounds someplace over where St. Louis is," I said, "someplace under those buildings, but the mounds got leveled, all their bones and pots and things dispersed somewhere. Maybe some of the mounds were where Forest Park is. That big Louisiana Centennial World's Fair was headquartered in the park and where Washington University is now. They had Geronimo here as a prisoner of war, they posed him in a 1904 opentop car, in a top hat holding the steering wheel."

"Man, how'd you like to be a traffic cop that pulled *him* over?" my brother said.

"They had a lot of people here, Filipinos of some kind I think. Old Teddy Roosevelt came and talked, so I've heard or read, about how America was now getting the right control of the Pacific and giving freedom to the Philippines from the corrupt and decadent Europeans or maybe just the corrupt and decadent Spanish, Cuba and all that, bringing oppressed people under the American imperium or whatever. Not even the Pacific Ocean could stop our westward expansion. Columbus would have felt vindicated—right on to China and India, Teddy!"

"You think the Indian mounds were over by the university?"

"Some not far from where my classrooms are. I might be teaching where they had their signal fires or sacrificial smokes. You could probably see any of that from right here on this big mound. I don't know whether mounds across the river were rivals of this place or settlements and outposts."

"They might have just been friends and allies," Aaron said. "But where did they all go? What happened, did they just die out or move away or what?"

"Nobody seems to know," I said. "I don't care what they say, though, my view is that things fell apart for them just about when the Siouan peoples were passing westward and southward through here and splitting up. I mean the bunch that turned into our five peoples, the Dhegiha Siouan people that got to be the Ponca and Omaha that went up the Missouri to Nebraska and Dakota, and the Osage and Kaw that were in Missouri and Kansas, and the Quapaw that went down toward Arkansas."

"What's the evidence, though?" Addison asked. "I mean do you just think that because you'd like to believe it, or what?"

"Well, I've actually seen a passage in one of the Osage ceremonies that La Flesche recorded which to me seems to show contact between Osages and these Cahokia Mound people. The ceremony says, *then we joined the people of death and moved to another country.* We may have got some of our astronomical clan-orderings and ceremonial patterns from these Mound People right here where the three greatest rivers of this continent come together."

"You know," Kim said, "I can see the Arch from here and some of those St. Louis buildings, but I never saw this mound when we were up in the Arch. I wonder if you really could see us standing here, if you tried."

"Maybe," I said. "I think the Arch was made as a kind of gunsight that you look through towards the west, though."

"Maybe it's a one-way mirror," Aaron said.

"That's weird," Kim said.

"Got to get back, kids," I said. We crammed back into the car and maneuvered out again onto the freeway and drove back past the sloughs full of ducks and redwing blackbirds and cattails nodding. We drove smoothly on high-banked asphalt roads which twine and wrestle like cobras and spit their traffic into St. Louis. We drove past great waste-mounds and raw landfills out of which the stainless Gateway Arch was Frankenstein-stitched together, through the fragrance of ruined steel mills, of plastic plants, refineries for gasoline and herbicides. The bobsled-run of concrete highways ricocheted us into and through East St. Louis. My brother, looking out his window, said, "Did you see that TV documentary on this place? Is it as bad as the documentary said?"

"Yes and no," I said. "They showed all the buildings falling apart, they let people see a little of how our racist history set up this site to dump stockyard waste and industrial waste, and supply servants for rich St. Louis suburbs and all that. What they missed was the music and poetry, the people, everything that's maybe starting to happen now. They saw the corruption but had no idea of what hope is here if you look and listen. There's poets here, the salt has not lost its savor. You know how bad it was when you and I and all of our dysfunctional family were growing up in Oklahoma, you know the well-off people living around us could have written a documentary on how bad things were for us and how the statistics showed we would be nothing but a burden on society and anybody associated with us. Yet what are we doing now? Here you are, a Naval Defense mathematician and computer expert, here I am a college teacher. We paid a price, we'll go on paying it, but by God our family did not go down, not quite, not all of us all the time. There's strong people doing good things here in East St. Louis right while the media are showing the rest of it. People go around eating apples off the same tree they say has rotten limbs. You should have heard the people reading poems last May at the East St. Louis Community College. People don't stop breathing because the media say they died."

"Yeah, but crime doesn't go away just because a bunch of people are writing poems and reading them to each other. Washington D.C.'s a mess," my brother said.

"Name me a city anywhere that is *not* a mess. London's a mess. What I saw of Naples didn't look too good. All the rivers in the world are dirty with what comes from the cities that saddle the rivers. People have got to clean the rivers so they can wash themselves clean, so they can drink the water again. They may want to think the bad stuff is all on one side of the river but hell it's on both sides and in the river too. Look at that water down there!"

"Wow, look at how it roils around," Kim said. "I'd hate to try swimming in those eddies."

"It looks like it's pumping iron," Aaron said.

"It does, it really does!" Kim said. "That floating driftwood's like tattoos on the Mississippi's chest."

So we drove on over the elevated road and safely back into our suburb's green cooler shade, but I kept seeing in the rear-view mirror the Arch's steely shimmer. And that night going to bed it occurred to me to think again about how from Cahokia Mound we saw St. Louis, far off but clear, those sleek glass towers and the arch—but from the Arch itself we could not see Cahokia's mounds, let alone people standing on top of them. The Arch is a lot higher, six hundred and thirty feet, whereas the highest mound is not much over a hundred, and yet when we had gone up in the Arch and looked east from its windows, out over the Mississippi waters that come here from as far away as winds and seeds and people travel, we could not see the mounds or any people over there. As Indians, we saw St. Louis. As whites, we didn't see Cahokia. They had their ceremonies, those Indian people, their circles, they invited the sun and moon to come and look into the future for them. They surely couldn't have seen us in the future, the way we see them in the past. We had looked earlier this day into a dazzling eclipse, where the moon's shadow bit out a crumb of fire and made the world wear a strange light, showed us how frail the sun is, handled our personal star like an Oreo cookie, dark chocolate and sweet white. Chocolate, I was thinking, an Aztec word, they used it as royal drink—part of the sacred ball game, was it? Probably why pharmacologists named its alkaloid stimulant *theobromine,* food for the gods, because Mayans and Aztecs once handed it around on temple mounds in Mexico? We hand it around the household as a nightcap now, here where the great rivers meet, where their waters reflect on a shimmering steel Arch that will slowly, slowly fall into ruins, where this day we got together and watched a partial eclipse. Depends where you look from, a narrow stripe of chocolate shadow zipping across the earth, people outside it untouched by any difference in the light, but all the people it darkens made momentarily aware of being in the same weird place. Just for the moment they look into the passing stream and see all their faces together there, and then it fades.

PART TWO

Tribal Affairs

Making a Name

It's human names we think about, of course, when anyone first speaks of "naming." But everything we refer to has to have some name, and people who go by the Bible will speak of Adam's naming everything: as God formed each creature, it was brought before Adam (Gen. 2:19–20), and whatever Adam would call it, that would be its name. But among all these animals there was not found a helper and companion for Adam, so God created Eve out of Adam's rib, and then Adam gave HER the right generic name, which in English translates as "woman," explaining that (in Hebrew) this name implies that she was taken from "man" and is "bone of his bones and flesh of his flesh" (Gen. 2:20–23). Later, after the Fall, when God had decreed that she was to become the mother of all living humans, Adam named her "Eve." As for the name of Adam, he is referred to before the Fall simply as "the man": only after the Fall, when God is condemning him to till the earth and earn a living by the sweat of his brow, does the story refer to him as "Adam" (Gen. 3:17). In the Hebrew original, the names refer to their God-given roles as First Man and First Woman, as Parents, as Laborer and as Child-giver. The names have their Creation Story packed inside them like software, shaping their meanings and functions. Or, to take an older metaphor, their past and future beings are packed inside them as an oak is packed within an acorn.

The Judeo-Christian Creation Story fingers the primal human male as source of all names within human language—an authority given and confirmed by God himself, so that if anyone should ask "Why do we call an ant an ant? or a woman a woman? or one man Adam, one woman Eve?" there is a story to explain why, and it is a sacred story with the weight of God's own approval behind it. That is pretty much the way with Creation Stories and human language, particularly in their account of names for people or places or things or any creatures—though maybe not all Creation Stories are so patriarchal about the matter as the Hebrew account in Genesis.

But we do not live in biblical times, and our names are not linked so directly to divinity and authority, nor felt to have such absolute rightness and accuracy. To mention just a couple of matters not talked about in the Book of Genesis: in European societies—including the United States—property, status and power are closely tied to human names; and users of the English language are distanced from its vital center by certain features which (as will be shown) involve names. I want to talk about these matters a little, by way of meditation, not just because they are oddly patterned, but because their colorful surface covers a pulsing body of meaning. I'll begin with a less touchy area—the names of birds and plants—before moving into surnames and "Christian names" and marital settlements and legitimate heirs, and then into certain American places and their names.

Naming the Birds

Woodpeckers, of course, are birds which peck wood, and a redheaded woodpecker is one that has a red head. But what is a barn-swallow's favorite food, if not barns?[1] Maybe back in Anglo-Saxon days the official Bird-Namer happened to be asked to name Flycatchers first, and so later when he wanted the right metonym for *the Swallow that LIVES in barns and eats flying insects*, he couldn't name it for its favorite food, because the Flycatcher had already been given patent rights for that. Therefore he named this Swallow not for its eating habits but for its residential predilections—"BARNswallow, people, we'll call it a BARNSWALLOW, because that's where the critter lives!"; and the congregation responded: "Yea, verily: *vox populi est vox Dei.*"

I know that *swallow* as bird is very different from *swallow* as verb —I've looked up the etymologies, and I see it's uncertain whether the bird-name comes from the same pre-Germanic source as the verb-name. What I am playing with is how confusing, at first glance, our bird-names are. Some of them describe the bird they name, tell what it looks like (*bluejay*), what it does (*pied wagtail*), what it eats (*carrion crow*), how it sounds (*catbird*)—but others seem to be mere blobs of sound flipped onto a passing passerine, as for instance *sparrow* or *finch*. It's a fact that some of these sound-blobs were hi-fi records before time in our hot voice-boxes melted them out of shape: the Old English *cra* (whose cry told its name) became our modern *crow*, which does NOT say its name; and this change occurred as part of the Great Vowel Shift in the fifteenth century. So when King Alfred said *cra,* he sounded like one; when Queen Elizabeth said *crow* she was (I think) *an*-onomatopoetic—and in any case it was Greek to the crows.

But it isn't only the sounds that have gone off on us: the meanings, too, have faded from some of the names. How far (for instance) the Cardinal has fallen, whose name once linked him with the grandeur that was Rome, but now ties him to a secular St. Louis, by the waters of Mississippi, and the breweries of Busch! I wonder: was it his color—the red of a cardinal's robe—that got him his name as Cardinal Redbird? Certainly the bird-name "cardinal" is now just a convenient two or three syllables to drape over a persistent cheerful singing among new leaves, or a scarlet flutter among snowflakes.

Mostly, that is, the metaphors in common bird-names have slumped into obscurity, are no longer nominal poetry but mere sound-tags, for reference only. Granted, this is not true for some *literati*. Ornithologists still have the fun of naming in Latin and they tend to be outrageously figurative—dubbing the Redwinged Blackbird, for instance, *Agelaius phoeniceus phoeniceus*, to link its beautiful scarlet and gold epaulets to the legendary Phoenix. Even when not waxing mythic, they are apt to be vivid (the Sharpshinned Hawk is called *Accipiter velox velox*, which seems to translate as

"fast, FAST grabber"), sometimes with a tinge of egotism (the Eastern Henslow's Sparrow is called *Passerherbulus henslowi susurrans,*
"Henslow's whispering grass-sparrow").[2] But even such ornate Latin
fancies can't match the wit and imagination of "popular" names like
those found in older bird-books, where we learn that the Wood Ibis
has also been named *Gourd-head, Iron-head, Flint-head, Preacher,*
and *Spanish Buzzard,* while the Eastern Nighthawk is a.k.a. *Bull-
bat, Mosquito Hawk, Pork-and-Beans, Burnt-Land-Bird,* and *Chim-
ney Bat.*[3]

But those are all old names. I wonder whether we are still naming birds, and if so whether all the play and poetry have gone out
of naming them now. Once a single common name is hung round
its neck, and once a Latin "scientific" name is banded onto its feet,
custom piles such dust upon its name that the tongue hesitates to
touch it newly, and Juliet herself could not wish for a more arbitrary
linkage of name to namebearer. No one need think again of what's
in a bird's name, and the answer to a child's "What is THAT?" is
a syllable or two of sound totally disconnected from the language-
making powers at play in the questioning child. Instead of hearing
a small revelation, the child is handed a memory-tag, and has no
reason to hold the flutter of names as other than dis-figured, de-
mythicized, non-descript, mere tame and pinioned words that no
longer sing or soar from thought to sense and back.

Mysterious Greek Names

Now I'm going to take a leap in the dark and suggest that this is
not just an isolated area of English—thinking about how birds are
named may show us something about our language at large. It certainly *seems* to have only limited application, to involve only the
pleasant unbusinesslike minority of bird-watchers who like to get
up of a morning and hear the dinosaurs singing on their window-
sills.[4] Yet I think the way we name birds does illustrate a tendency of
English speakers that has grown even stronger since the days when
Chaucer poured so much French brandy into the mulled ale of his

English. This tendency is to disconnect English words from each other—to BORROW words for new meanings or new perceptions, rather than to CREATE "derived" forms or depend more heavily on extending by metaphor the old meanings to fit new things.

To illustrate from technological areas, when we invent a telephone we do not call it by an English term that would be "transparent" to everyone, such as FAR-SPEAKER; instead, we borrow the Greek elements TELE-, "far," and PHONE, "speak, speech." This ensures that any speaker who lacks Greek will have no clue that the newly borrowed word *telephone* is related to other words in English —the thing's name does not whisper to us that it helps us SPEAK AFAR. The black-box name makes this new piece of technology seem unrelated to ordinary speech, makes it mysterious, darkens knowledge. It suggests that technologists and scientists hold custody of our understanding, our speech, our culture. And of course it gives us a good reason for having our schools teach Latin and Greek as a way of promoting understanding, separating the elite few from the ignorant many. All this works to persuade ordinary speakers that only learned people—the scribes, the scientist-priests in white robes, the professors in black and blue and scarlet gowns— only THEY know what the language is really about. The rest of us are confined to the ordinary and common words, otherwise we just deal with words as we deal with the complicated new automobiles, black boxes of electronic power into whose innards only a priestly nerd may pry for auspices of bull or bear. In short, language is "mystified."[5]

The results of all this are not entirely negative; that is, class and status barriers provide certain kinds of benefits. By such classical or learned borrowing, English develops a huge vocabulary (neatly divided into class, professional, and status areas restricted to chosen speakers), which perhaps necessarily relies more on lexical meaning than on idiomatic nuancing, compared to languages with smaller vocabularies like French. Also, it may be easier to keep synonyms or related terms distinctly different in connotative range, if they do not resemble each other in sound and structure. This neat separation may allow terms thus differenced to go their own ways; the road forks, and each fork carries its traffic without jams or crashes, so to speak.

Think, for instance, of the various nuances and distinctions among the "ordinary English" terms *far-seeing, far-sighted,* and the Greek/Latin *telescopic, television,* and *presbyopic.* Each of these refers to some kind of seeing at a distance, but *far-seeing* is specialized, "fenced off" as it were, to refer to the kind of "vision" exercised by a prophet or someone looking into the future with care and "foresight," while *far-sighted* can refer either to someone whose eyes do not focus well on near objects, or to someone who sees well at a distance. *Far-sighted* in that first sense is a popular synonym for the medical term *presbyopic*—in which *presby-* comes from the Greek word meaning "old" and *-opic* from the Greek word for "eye." So *presbyopic* meant originally "old-eyed"—no doubt because human eyes tend to lose ability to focus on nearby things as we grow older.[6] As for *telescopic,* it is a perfectly ordinary and common word for us, but just like *telephone* it does not "tell" English speakers what it refers to, nor does *television.* Their common roots are hidden from our surface awareness.

As suggested above, such Greek and Latin suburbs of the urbane sprawl that is English do have their stately beauties, though they chain out the *hoi polloi* whose noses are not suited to the Olympian air of Classical Studies. Aristocracies can produce grand things, and the redlining of English by its word-origins into these status-hierarchies gives an appearance of precision and distinction that makes English a good place to live, a regular Noo Yawk, IF one has visas or licenses for all its subdivisions. Nevertheless, there is a price, which is to have the lexical rules of English seem arbitrary, capricious, inconsistent—in short, MYSTERIOUS and ONLY FOR THE PRIESTS TO KNOW, with no-go zones, places where our hesitant voices seem to invite being spreadeagled and frisked for fake ID/ideas.

Getting back to birds: looking at how we name them helped us see how "opaque" English is made by going abroad for its names. What, then, would a "transparent" language be like in its naming? The common English names for birds can help us see this. To call a Wood

Ibis a "Preacher" is to use metaphor transparently: the bird is tall, gaunt, solemn in appearance; it has a judgmental gaze, perches high and conspicuous above its "flock"—in short, the name is not only "transparent," it offers a stained-glass commentary on the stereotype of a Protestant pastor, and nobody needs a gloss on this commentary.

Looking for the Right Names

But what if naming was still an active process for those learning the language? We see what that might be like when we read Charles Eastman's fascinating *Indian Boyhood*, whose paperback reprint may still be found in many bookstores. Eastman, born about 1858, was raised, to the age of fifteen, among his Santee Sioux people — at first in Minnesota, then as a four-year-old fleeing with them into Canada after the massacres of 1862.[7] *Indian Boyhood*, published in 1902, is Eastman's account of his life to age 15, and describes in considerable detail how he was educated as an Indian. His uncle was in charge of this education, and when Eastman would leave the tepee each morning, would tell him to look well at everything he saw, and when Eastman returned, would "catechize [him] for an hour." One thing on which he catechized him is thus described by Eastman:

> It was his custom to let me name all the new birds that I had seen during the day. I would name them according to the color or the shape of the bill or their song or the appearance and locality of the nest . . . anything that impressed me as characteristic. He then usually informed me of the correct name. Occasionally I made a hit and this he would warmly commend.[8]

Eastman's account shows us that among the Santee, a boy of eight or ten could be sent out to invent a name for each bird he saw, and sometimes his name would turn out to be exactly the one used by the tribe for that bird. This seems extremely unlikely for a speaker of English, where so many names are not evidently descriptive or figurative. Yet it is surely the case that humans, if their language is not so enclaved as English is, will develop similar figurative or de-

scriptive terms for what they observe. We can easily imagine a boy
going out and seeing what we call a bluebird, and returning to report he had seen a BLUE BIRD. Of course, given its red-orange belly
and white underparts, he could plausibly call it a *red-white-and-blue
bird*, or (reaching a bit) an *American-flag-bird*, or even (if it were
Bastille Day) a *Tricolor-bird*. Eastman's account shows that among
Santee speakers this was possible with ALL the birds. Learning their
names was part of learning to look closely, observe precisely, report
accurately. No doubt an Osage Indian boy, if sent out to look at insects and name them, might have come back and reported that he
had seen a *ni-dse-thi tonga*, "big-yellow-rump," and his uncle would
realize he meant a "bumblebee"—for which that is the Osage word,
according to Francis La Flesche.[9]

And Naming Machines

But English is still relatively "transparent" wherever things ARE
still being named by and for the general community of speakers—
an activity now less likely to involve birds than machines. Think
for instance of *cars, automobiles* (those terms are from Latin and
Greek, though *car* seems to have been borrowed into Latin from
Celtic): how many terms we have, few of them Latin or Greek, for
new kinds of car—*hatchbacks, hotrods, limos, vans, coupes, four-
doors, trucks, pickups, tankers, Smokeys, beetles, junkers, semis,
buses*, to name a very few of very many. And think of the flying creatures we have made: *jets, fighters, space shuttles, smart rocks, red-
eye specials*, all sorts of winged words for winged machines newly
made for our namers to break a champagne syllable over. Think, too,
of the *Fuzzbusters* and *think-tanks* and *interfacings*, of *software* and
Silicon Valley, or of *booting up computers*—and how about *laptops*
and *notebooks* and all such new terms for new things? Some of these
new terms are invented or twisted into their applications by the in-
ventors themselves; many other terms come from the people using
the inventions. Wherever the mass of people need a new word, they
make a compound (laptop), or use an old term figuratively (shuttles,

pods, smart rocks and brilliant pebbles). This is true not only where machines are involved, but for *any* area of craft or business or way of making a living.

Well, now that I think of it, it may not be true of SOME crafts: I don't know of a single word coined for English by English professors or departments of literature, not lately anyhow. The Pentagon, and the auto industry, computer craft, politicos and ad-people, bureaucrats and teenagers, all hail new words down like a thunderstorm in May, but we professors are dry as the Dust Bowl in August, more apt to spray Agent Orange upon new word-growths than spread compost around them. I still remember from long years ago the bit of Pentagonese quoted in a column by Jack Anderson. While the Bay of Pigs invasion was in the planning phase (Anderson reported), the Pentagon was highly skeptical of the CIA's enthusiastic forecasts, but nobody wanted to say openly that it would fail. So they protected themselves by sending out a series of memos expressing— cautiously, and vaguely—doubts and worries. Thus did they do what Anderson said was known among military bureaucrats as "digging a paper foxhole." Delectable phrase—I wish my literary colleagues had invented it! I suspect we do coin words, in actual speech around the departmental halls and lunchrooms, but we "know better" than to write them down—after all, for English professors, spoken English is throwaway, not keeper stuff.

Getting Personal

Now a question so far untouched: what about our own "personal" names? I know it is possible to look up the "original" meanings of, say, *Theodore* or *Dorothy*, and find that both mean "gift of God." I know it is possible to show that many of our "surnames" or "family names" come from earlier crafts and occupations (*Baker, Wheelwright, Carter, Smith, Fletcher*—a maker of arrows, one who put the feathers on), or places (*Lincoln, Shannon, Revard*), or from appearance (*White, Black, Brown, Whitehead, Long, Short*). I know many names are biblical and link their bearers to history and ultimately to the Hebrew Creation Story. I know many Jews were forcibly re-named in Germany before or during the Hitler regime, and I know many people have both an ethnic or religious "true name" and a civil or outward "legal name." There are nicknames which may point to personal history or professional achievements or parental malfea-sance—which is to say, each nickname carries a real story about the person so named, a story that the name-givers thought important enough to make every address to this person carry a reminder of that story.

And yet, and yet! when I ask students in a class I teach on Ameri-can Indian Literature to tell me about names, and what their par-ticular names "do" for them, I always get from them just accounts implying that a name is a way of individualizing the person named, as if individualizing were the whole of becoming a person. Almost never does a student see, at first, that the network of names links those who are named to a whole social system, to a religious struc-ture. (Even if that "family tree" of religion is "dead," as when a stu-dent claims to be an atheist or to have renounced the family faith, much still lives in its hollow trunk and leafless branches—things come out at night to their dreaming selves from that religious back-ground and sing old songs with the dreamers.) We seem carefully cued to believe, in American society, that names are JUST personal or, at most, familial, not SOCIAL. Our whole society is taught to be-lieve that a *Julia Doe* is unique, that the name merely lets us know who is being singled out, when in fact the name usually genders the person named, echoes nationality, hints at ethnicity, suggests religion, and of course allows Social Security benefits, international travel (passport, that is), inheritance rights—and, for a good many years, has keyed marital status for women.

What, then, of our "full legal" names—those we must carry on "identity" cards, those we must show are legally ours, before we can legally inherit, or bequeath? We *are* expected, it is true, to have unique personal names, and since human population exploded in the nineteenth and twentieth centuries, this has meant in Euro-pean culture that each person needs a unique combination of several names. We *are* expected to have a "family" name, which shows we are "legitimate" and can legally inherit from our true parents. Also, in American naming custom, we have a "first" name (often called a "Christian" name until fairly recently), and very often a "middle" name. These first and middle names are supposed to be given purely according to the wishes or whims of the parents, but as we all know they often link us to older family members. And just to spell out a little more the religious dimension, in certain sects there are ceremonial linkages for these names—they may for instance "belong" to saints of the Catholic church, thus linking the named person to the stories and the power of a martyr or virgin or teacher. Once that linkage is established it takes the named person back through time to the founder of the religion, that is (in the Catholic way), Jesus Christ; and then still further, back to the Jewish Creation Story, which Jesus (according to Christians) reauthenticated in his version of that religion. So names in Christian culture do point back through many ways to the Creation Story, just as we see is true for Osages, for instance.[10]

But there are too many of "us" to be sure of having unique names with only three or four "name-slots" to fill—which is why American names are turning now into numbers. A Social Security number is needed whenever one is to receive a fee or wage "personal names" are not enough, because there are too many Thomas Jefferson Smiths and John Hernandez Does. It is startling to think that in the early days of telephones, one simply picked up the speaker and asked for a particular person, and the "operator" could put one through. The assigning of a unique NUMBER to each person makes excellent sense—and yet I wonder what this means. Numbers don't have stories, at least not out in the open. Numbers are precisely what we use when we want to ignore all possible differences between, say, a thousand spiders and a thousand bridal nights, and want to talk about only the properties of the number one thousand. "Mathematics," Bertrand Russell remarked, "is that occupation in which we do not know what we are talking about, nor whether what we are saying is true." We have so many children now that we have to use numbers to talk about them; urban shoes make forgetful mothers.

Naming America: "Amherst"

But so far we have not looked at our signpost names, those which tell us where we live, where we come from, where we are headed. Let's move, then, from persons to places, from individual to national and international—let's look briefly at what we call the places where we live, between name and number. What looks redeyed from under the campus of a college, the cemeteries of our dead warriors, the asphalt parking lots, urine-drenched projects, photogenic penthouses of our shining cities on their hills?

Let me start with a meditation on the name of a New England college town, and what lies beneath that name. It's an attractive little place in north-central Massachusetts called Amherst, named for Jeffery, Lord Amherst, who was a British military commander in the "French and Indian Wars" of the eighteenth century. The main branch of the University of Massachusetts is located on the north side of Amherst, and Amherst College (prestigious and expensive Little Ivy League place) on its south side. Amherst is famous, among literary types, as the home town of Emily Dickinson, whose father and brother were important officers and trustees of Amherst College, and while I was teaching at Amherst College in the late 1950s you could still smell their family scandals but you would hear only tight-lipped silences about them, the scandals not yet in print, because the mongering of them was not yet so fiercely driven by academic publish-or-perish insanity.

But why exactly is the *town* called Amherst? Of course, it is named FOR a particular man, Jeffery, Lord Amherst—but why for *him*, of all people? Well, let me slip into this mystery by a back way, cloaked in a little "personal" anecdote.

When Robert Frost, who had long been a faculty member of Amherst College, would come through town for his annual Chapel talk and poetry reading, it was usual for him to be brought out to the house of an English faculty member and sit around explaining the world as it appeared to the greatest living writer of poetry in English. As a young instructor, I listened in on a couple of these occasions and was richly entertained. In one of these sessions, someone remarked that I was not only from Oklahoma but was part Osage Indian, and when Frost learned this he immediately told me his very first poem had been written, when he was in high school and reading Parkman's history of Mexico, on the Indian side of the matter, against Cortez and the Conquistadores, and for Montezuma.[11] A little polite sparring followed this, because I knew that another Frost poem, "The Vanishing Red," hardly shows a pro-Indian handling of its events and characters: its main character, a malevolent miller, waits until the dumb Indian who has come gawking around the mill's machinery is hanging right over the dangerous part, and then shoves the Indian into the machinery, where of course he "vanishes."

The poem, though powerful and disturbing, is neither anti-Indian nor pro-Indian; rather, like Frost's macabre "Out, Out . . ." it is a bleak and Hardyesque piece, speaking to the way technology and European proprietors nastily helped Indians vanish, abetted by a conspiracy of silence. Grim, but accurate history—and granted that Frost shows this Indian as stupid, his poems are full of non-Indians being clobbered for clumsy ignorance of social codes and procedures. True, there is considerable difference between being covered with a load of hay and shamed, as happens to a non-Indian in "The Code," and being pushed to one's death in steel machinery, as happens to "The Vanishing Red." Yet in "The Code," the man who forked that load of hay onto the code-breaking farmer "meant" murder, and the poem's narrator implies that had the offender been smothered to death, the witnesses would have regarded him as deserving it. This poet sometimes casts a cold eye on life and death.

To me, then, that Amherst evening gave serious pleasure, so far as my few exchanges with Frost were concerned. I had profound respect for him, and far too great admiration for the subtlety and magnificence of his poems to worry whether one among them was what—as a human being not wanting Indian people to be slurred—I would have preferred it to be. I had no quarrel with Robert Frost's writing about Indians, or far less than I have with Shakespeare's writing about Welshmen and Irishmen. There was another reason, though, why the question of Indians in relation to Amherst was a ticking package in the room just then. The package was labeled "tenure," and it was addressed to me, in care of the English Department. By then I had come to know that the department's major power wanted me out and would prevail—and being thus ostracized where I sat, I took this Indian question as oddly relevant. Asserting myself to be Indian had been a part—small, a mere pea under forty mattresses of departmental considerations—of what set me off from those who *would* get tenure. I had clearly, and not just casually, presented myself as Oklahoman and Indian, in ways that made me seem unsuitable to the shrewd old Scotch bull of that department, who had sat silent but focused like a burning glass on my brief back-and-forth with Frost.

It wasn't only the question of Frost's Indian poems. Once, that night, somebody referred to the College's official song, which has a line about how Lord Jeffery "fought the Indians," and I said I objected to that line, that it did not seem to me the college should keep that line in a song the students were taught to sing. I glanced from the amused face of Robert Frost over to the unamused scowl of the departmental power, and I saw more clearly why I would be leaving Amherst: not only was I unsuited to them, but they to me. My little exchange about Lord Amherst was filed carefully, I supposed, with the fact that I had once asked mildly (when someone mentioned to me that the town of Deerfield a few miles north of Amherst was where a notorious massacre by Indians had occurred) why in the world those Indians would want to attack a town of people, just for settling on their hunting grounds. And very likely neither exchange seemed of real importance to those listening: they were just a tiny part of reasons why the town and college and I were not really suited for each other, did not fit, rubbed the wrong ways, smelled mutually bad.

It could have been worse. I had heard, even then, of how Jeffery had fought the Indians—with smallpox-infected blankets, at times—but on that evening, I did not throw that particular red blanket in front of the departmental bull. I think that I actually doubted, at that time, whether the accusation was well documented; I vaguely recall that some Amherst person with historical credentials had assured me it was probably a slander. Since then, I have seen reputable scholarly assertions that Lord Amherst called for the use of smallpox germs against the Indians, though I have not myself researched the documentation for those assertions.[12]

So under the name set upon that beautiful little town with its lovely college, magnificent poets, splendid students, extremely able teachers, there was a buried history of ethnic cleansing, carried out with the help of germ warfare, that was an important part of the British aristocracy's fight for imperial dominance against the French aristocracy. The town, and the college, had been given this name precisely *because* that particular English lord *had* fought the Indians. Within this "mere school song" of gentleman scholars from clean families, there was direct reference to that history, and not to support the singing of it was to take a different view of New England history, of American history. Only a churl, only someone born and brought up in Indian Territory, would have the tactless gall to so much as hint at these things. I do wonder whether that might possibly have been one glittering thought in the brilliant old mind of Robert Frost, friend of Montezuma, when at the evening's end he turned in the doorway, put up a hand with palm out, and said to me, "Goodnight—*Indian!*" I am glad, because his poems have been and are part of the bright side of this universe for me, that I did not answer with like irony, though I nearly did: "Good night—*Yankee!*"

Naming America: "St. Louis"

It should not be thought, however, that moving from *Amherst* to *St. Louis* has changed things at all. I think all the European names set upon this Promised Land scutcheon a history of heroic achievement *and* human pain. The French king Louis IX, for whom St. Louis city was named, surely did good deeds every day, helped old people across the Mediterranean or whatever. I am perfectly willing to let him be praised among citizens of the pleasant town bearing his name, in which I have lived since 1961. We need not consider what a Crusade was, rehearse the pros and cons of Muslim expansions and Christian reconquests, rethink the history of Europe before 1492. Past history, as they say—that's how they were, over *there*.

And yet, one more point is worth mention *here*. In the years

1836–40, there was a terrible smallpox epidemic among Indians over almost the whole territory between the Rockies and the Mississippi, striking up into Canada and Alaska, and westward into California. About this, a recent authoritative discussion says, "Certainly, the distribution of smallpox-infected blankets by the U.S. Army to Mandans at Fort Clark, on the Missouri River in present-day South Dakota, was the causative factor in the pandemic of 1836–40," adding that the blankets were taken from a U.S. Army infirmary in St. Louis—which, I assume, was the one at Jefferson Barracks.[13] Named for Thomas Jefferson, these barracks are where the dragoons were quartered when (in the 1830s) they were first sent out to St. Louis to conduct the "Indian Wars."

So, having left the New England place named for an English lord who "fought the Indians," I had come to a Midwestern place (*Gateway to the West,* as St. Louisans call it) named for a French saint who "fought the Saracens": a place from which American presidents "fought the Indians" with exactly the same civilized means as had Lord Amherst. Something else: Missouri (unlike Massachusetts) has no Indian reservations within its borders, because all "aboriginal rights" were extinguished within this slaveholding state precisely during the 1830s, when smallpox germs and dragoons were being sent out to destroy all barriers between the new American republic and its manifest destiny of controlling the continent.

The will and various ways to accomplish this ethnic cleansing had been shown soon after the American president, Jefferson, in 1803 "acquired" Missouri from the French dictator, Napoleon, as part of the Louisiana Purchase, a transaction carried out without any negotiations with Osages and other native peoples who had long occupied much of Missouri and particularly the St. Louis area.[14] Americans at once paid mercenaries from other Indian nations to come and attack the Osages and other Missouri Indians so as firmly to impose the new American order.[15] Pierre Laclede, who established the town of St. Louis in the 1760s just after Lord Amherst had fought the (French and) Indians, had sent his trappers and traders out among the Osages to intermarry and carry on trade. One such Frenchman was Joseph Revard, whose half-Osage son would later operate the first trading post in what is now Oklahoma—where, in 1821, he was killed by Cherokees who had been crossing the Mississippi as a result of American pressures on them in their home territories in Georgia, Alabama and Tennessee, pressures which escalated in the 1830s to drive them along the Trail of Tears into Oklahoma.

For New England and Amherst, the 1830s must have been a time of peaceful acquisition of fertile and beautiful estates. Even as the smallpox plague was killing Indians west of the Mississippi, and the Trail of Tears was being followed by Indians of the southeastern states, the literary and cultural flowering of New England was under way. Think of the *Tanglewood Tales,* or the stories of Hawthorne and Melville that evoke the beautiful country of western Massachusetts in the Berkshires, where if you drive today you will see roadside signs of inns "established in 1763" or later. Emerson, Hawthorne, Melville, Longfellow, Thoreau, Whittier, Lowell dwelt in a Promised Land of milk and honey, if also of considerable snow and ice. They, like Fenimore Cooper to the south and west, could afford to speak well of the Indians their British grandparents had "displaced," could remember with pleasure where the names of Massachusetts and Connecticut came from, could give Tashtego and Hiawatha honorable roles in their fiction and poetry, could point the finger of blame at crude and cruel other Americans who held slaves, who mistreated Indian women and children. Jeffery, Lord Amherst had held an English title anathema to American republicans, but he had fought the Indians, and the town and college owed him a debt, paid by taking his name, honoring his reputation, denying those blanket slanders. And, of course, a pity about the Indians.

I wonder how New England students in those days read certain books of the *Aeneid*—those in which Aeneas travels up the Tiber to negotiate alliance, or favorable neutrality, with Evander. I wonder because Virgil seems to me to use Evander, in book eight, almost exactly as the New Englanders used Indians. Evander, when Aeneas reaches him, reveals that his own ancestors came from Arcadia, acknowledges that he and Aeneas share distant relatives, and not only welcomes Aeneas to Italy but shows him around the now-wild scenes over which the future Rome will be built, and where Evan-

der's own people and he will be literally buried by the new empire
Aeneas will found.[16] Was it by murdering Brer Remus that Romu-
lus gave Rome his own name? And then there is also the matter of
Rome's Capitol building, underneath which the skull marks those
old deaths on which the new empire must be founded. Perhaps
under every nation's governing buildings, under every place name
of a new nation, that skull is buried. CapitOlism is our way of life.

And Making Good Names

But I don't want to leave matters there. To name a place, to keep
steadily before us the history that went into its naming, is not to
be finished with it, no matter what wretched or heroic actions once
happened there. We are making history now, burning sweetgrass
over the old names. For several years I served as a board member of
the American Indian Center of Mid-America in St. Louis, and each
September our Center has put on an annual Plains Indian Powwow
in Jefferson Barracks Park, at the southern tip of St. Louis looking
out on the Mississippi River. What this means is that every September, Indians from all over America dance round the drum on springy
grass that grows just where the barracks were built to control us,
where the hospital's blankets were fixed to kill us. Where we dance
is not far from the Veterans' Cemetery in this park—some of whose
buried warriors are Indian, some not.

   We don't just dance. Our American Indian Center of Mid-America
has dealt with the problems and ministered to the life and on-
going activities of several thousand American Indians living in the
metropolitan area of St. Louis. Comanche, Osage, Ponca, Omaha,
Kiowa, Caddo, Choctaw, Cherokee, Navajo, Hidatsa, Otoe-Missouri,
Tohono O'odham, Houma, Delaware, Yaqui, Pawnee, Seminole,
Creek, Dogrib, Zuni, Apache, Laguna, Shawnee, Lakota, Seneca,
Oneida, Mohawk, Chippewa—these and other peoples live, work,
play, dance at our powwows, have sent their children to our Crafts
Circles to learn their skills, use our food pantries, find help in
family emergencies, come to our Talking Circle, keep the old ways
alive into this new age.

Think, after all, of where we got this name *American Indian*—
from *Amerigo* Vespucci and from *India:* an Italian explorer, an Asian
subcontinent. Strange, wrong, impossible, but we let those names be
hung around us. And just as we made exquisite medicine pouches or
moccasins by working onto skins the beads Europeans "gave" us, so
also we may continue to make beautiful our inward understanding
of such outward names. Dying animals gave us these skins, dying
humans gave us these names, beneath and upon them are the losses
and sacrifices of those who gave us life, now we can wear them in
beauty, make them tell who we are and how we came to be here,
put our bodies and our spirits into these names, pass them on to our
children when we go. We are still making, still giving our names—
wherever they come from, we will take them around the drum.
When the songs rise and the people dance, when our own names are
called at the drum, there old and new names too may be heard. We
will gather, we will recognize each other, we will have a good time
till the dance is over and then, we hope, we will once again go safely
back to our homes in a land that is named, for now, America.

History, Myth, and Identity
among Osages and Other Peoples

Something strange appears when we look at certain autobiographies of Indian people: the notion of identity, of how the individual is related to world, people, self, differs from what we see in "Euroamerican" autobiography. In "Western Civilization," an *identity* is something shaped between birth and death, largely by tiny molecules called genes, somewhat also by what the child's nervous system undergoes between birth and the first few years thereafter—and with every year past the first one, events become less and less important in shaping that identity.[1] That is not how Geronimo sees his identity in the autobiography he dictated to S. M. Barrett.[2] Nor does Geronimo begin by focusing on what a Euroamerican audience would likely consider the key to his identity: the clash with American soldiers and invaders of the Apache lands.[3] Geronimo does not even get around to mentioning his own birth until the book's third chapter. Instead, he begins the story of his life in this way: "In the beginning the world was covered with darkness. There was no sun, no day. The perpetual night had no moon or stars. There were, however, all manner of beasts and birds. . . . All creatures had power of speech and were gifted with reason. There were two tribes of creatures, the birds and . . . the beasts."[4] Geronimo then tells how the birds wanted light brought into the world, but the beasts would not have it, and there was war. The birds won, admitting light and so allowing humans to live and thrive. But the Dragon continually came down and devoured human children, until one year a son of the Rainstorm was born to the woman, and she hid her son away until he grew up to fight and kill the Dragon.[5] This boy's name was *Apache*, which (Barrett's book says) literally means *Enemy*, and he was the first chief of the people, first to wear the eagle's feathers in sign of justice, wisdom, and power such as the birds had shown in fighting for light. For Apache and his people, *Usen* created a homeland, placing within it, as in each homeland created for a people, all that was best for them: grain, fruits, game, herbs of healing, a pleasant climate, all that they could use for clothing and shelter. Geronimo concludes this opening part of his autobiography by saying, "Thus it was in the beginning: the Apaches and their homes each created for the other by Usen himself. When they are taken from these homes they sicken and die. How long until it is said, there are no Apaches?"[6] It is only after this Genesis-like history of his world's creation, his people's creation and deliverance, of their land's creation, of why they are called *Apaches*, of what it means to be taken from the land created particularly for his people, that Geronimo speaks of himself—of his individual birth into the world: "I was born in No-doyohn Canyon, Arizona, June, 1829."[7]

Whatever the order of importance among such facts might be for a Euroamerican autobiography, Geronimo ranked them from cosmic through geologic to tribal, subtribal, family and then only, last and in full context, the "individual" self that was Geronimo. And every *name* in his narrative, whenever he speaks it, has its symbolic meaning that resonates in this deeper context, can be rightly understood only in light of that part of the people's history which he is then telling. *Apache* does not "mean" only what (in Barrett's version) it "literally says," *Enemy*, but refers to The Enemy of that Dragon who threatens human children, and it is the name of the first great "Culture Hero" (as Euroamericans would call him: that Son of the Rainstorm who killed the Great Destroyer of Humankind.

I doubt that for most Euroamericans our national terms—*English, American, German, European*—resonate thus, because we lack a system of national and personal names that is openly and plainly

linked to our mythic history or religious creeds.[8] There is of course
the Catholic custom of naming after saints and biblical figures, and
the Jewish naming arrangements that preserve religious and ethnic
and family histories, and there are certainly subterranean passages
between mainstream American personal names and the older familial and ethnic and national histories hidden within them. Yet
particularly among Protestants, it seems, Americans have untied
their names and individual histories from place and nation to an astonishing extent in the last five hundred years—precisely since the
terms *individualism, self, identity* and *civilize* came into the English language in their current meanings.[9]

Now, when Geronimo told his life story, he had been a prisoner
of war for twenty years, and a great deal had been done to *civilize* him.[10] As a recent editor of his autobiography puts it, "He took
on all the trappings of the white man's civilization, becoming a
farmer, a member of the Dutch Reformed Church, a Sunday School
teacher, and a tireless promoter of himself, hawking photographs,
bows and arrows at various fairs and expositions."[11] Civilized or not,
Geronimo at seventy-six years of age (when dictating his life story
to Barrett) still had his culture, his hierarchy of values. He knew
who he was and where he came from, and he was sure that removal
of the Apaches from their *homeland* meant, for him and for all of
them, the loss not just of a "way of life" or a "home," but a change
in, perhaps a loss of, their *beings*—or, as we might say, their *identi-
ties.* In his story, the notions of cosmos, country, self, and home are
inseparable.

The result of losing that *homeland* can be seen in another Apache
autobiography, though at first it seems to offer counter-evidence on
the relation of being to land. This is a book narrated by one of the
young Apache men who went with Geronimo on one of the last
breakaways into the free Sierra Madre of Mexico—a man named
Jason Betzinez, born in 1860 and producing his autobiography in
1958 (he died in 1960, aged 100, from a car crash).[12] Betzinez tells us
that in 1902, when the Apache heads of families met with military
authorities at Fort Sill, Oklahoma (where they were still prisoners
of war), to request once more that they be repatriated to their old

homeland in New Mexico, as they had been promised when they surrendered in Mexico, Betzinez himself stood up courageously and said that he wanted to stay in Oklahoma:

> I was born and raised among these Indians. I lived just like they did—a hard life, *homeless and hopeless.* But through a Government school I had a chance to *better myself.* . . . I learned to be a blacksmith. I worked in a steel mill. I learned farming. Now I am being forced to choose between this new, good life and that old, primitive life out west. If I go west to live in a camp as a reservation Indian, all that I have gained, all that I have learned, will be lost. . . . My wish this day is that the Government should give me a house and land and permit me to remain. (p. 190)

Betzinez was clearly a fine person, and I would bet my life he was a good neighbor and friend—but the quoted words make him seem a perfect instance of a "wild" Indian who was "tamed" by the Euroamerican schools. Indeed, rebutting an Arizona senator, Betzinez says this himself: "At the time the removal of the Apaches from Fort Sill was . . . under consideration in Washington. One of the Senators from Arizona said, 'You can no more tame an Apache than you can a rattlesnake.' I think   the recent history of our people flings those words back in the worthy gentleman's teeth" (p. 199). At the age of twenty-seven, Jason Betzinez had been put into Carlisle Indian School, taught to speak and write English, converted to Christianity, and brought to be ashamed of and hostile to Apache dances and ceremonies, and now he considered his Apache life as "the old pitiful existence to which I was born" (p. 153).

Consider how different Betzinez's "old" life had been from Geronimo's. Geronimo had been born in 1829 and could grow up both "wild" and "free"; Betzinez, born in 1860 after the U. S. annexed his homeland, was from his teens onward under deadly and constant harassment. As he tells it, "As far back as I remember we had never had a permanent home or a place we could call our own. Some of us were beginning to prefer quiet and security to the ever present worry and fear of being hounded. . . . I think we realized dimly, as we jolted along in these wagons, that even as prisoners our worst troubles

might be coming to an end" (p. 141). The episode he refers to here is
when the Apaches, having been rounded up in Mexico and Arizona,
were being railroaded off to Florida as prisoners of war, in direct
violation of the agreement made when they surrendered. What Betzinez says, in effect, is that the prisoners have decided they are only
safe in prison. It is meant, of course, as compliment to the jailers.

It is a hard question whether Geronimo or one of the older
Apaches, if asked to describe Jason Betzinez when he returned from
Carlisle to live at Fort Sill in 1900, would have described him
as "Apache." His *identity* was not merely changed from "wild" to
"tame," from hunter/warrior to blacksmith/farmer. Consider: it was
thenceforward impossible for Betzinez to begin his life story with
the Apache account of the Creation, for he was now a sincere Christian. It was no longer relevant to his life to name the subtribes
of Apaches as Geronimo's autobiography does, for readers of Betzinez's story would be interested only in his being "an Apache." After
going to Carlisle, Jason Betzinez had no homeland unless the United
States government assigned him one. He had no religion shared
with his people, no ceremonies that tied his youth to his age or self
to tribe. In short, he had no IDENTITY unless he could reinvent
himself in Euroamerican terms.

After 1900, that is, he was cut off completely from his first twenty-
six years of life—from cosmos, tribe, homeland, and "values." From
that time on, *all that made him Indian was his race*—and the chief
test of that, by Euroamerican values, would be whether he could
raise his status to be like a "white" man, for that alone would show
whether he was racially inferior or could "make it." His sense of
worth now depended on how NON-Apache he could act. Yet, of
course, skin color and features would "identify" him as "Indian," no
matter what his lifestyle became.

Betzinez had kept some attitudes, and he saw clearly how false
was some of what Euroamericans wanted him to believe about his
people's history. He could see it because he still had, in oral history, Apache truths that were omitted or distorted by printed Euroamerican accounts; he makes this clear at the very beginning of his
autobiography (pp. 1–2). He quickly reveals that even though he had

come to praise the non-Apache life to which Carlisle had turned him, even though he deplored the wish of "wild" Apaches to return to an existence and home country which, he insisted, was wretched and harassed, yet his feelings and memories of that homeland and existence were not negative. On the contrary, as he says: "We loved this beautiful land. . . . Between . . . 1858, when the Government granted us this reservation 'forever,' and 1876, when that same Government took it away from us forever so that white men seeking gold might have it, we lived there in peace and contentment. We hunted, gathered and traded. . . . For a short time life was . . . a happy one" (p. 25). But the official views expressed as Betzinez concludes his autobiography are very different from those at his beginning. From his Carlisle days, Betzinez had "thrown away" his Apache identity and accepted the Euroamerican self patterned for him by the soldiers at Carlisle whom he came to admire and trust. It is a remarkable and attractive self, clearly that of an unusually strong, courageous and decent man, whose life is told in this book. But it is clearly a Euroamerican self. We may account for its shaping, perhaps, by the imprisonment, penances, and education at Carlisle. If this were a U.S. citizen in 1994 we would presumably call the process brainwashing.

How, then, do we account for the different sense of self or identity in Geronimo's book? Here we have no clear description from Geronimo: he shows us an Apache self, but does not show how it was shaped. We can look into particular books for some idea of the ways Apache education shaped people—for instance, Morris Opler's *Apache Odyssey, Journey Between Two Worlds* tells how a Mescalero Apache "grew to maturity when his people . . . were experiencing defeat, confinement, and profound cultural readjustment."[13] But something more than one tribe's self-shaping is involved here, or so it appears to me from some years of having taught a course in which we read autobiographies of Indians from very different tribal cultures. Not only how Apache but how Indian beings are shaped is what I want to look into, if only a little way, in this chapter. One trail into this great Sierra is the way of naming and using language.

The autobiography that has helped me see how naming and language reflect and shape a sense of identity within the world, both outside and part of an Indian self, is Charles Eastman's *Indian Boyhood*.[14] Eastman was a Santee Sioux born about 1858 and raised, like Geronimo, "wild," but Eastman was then "brought in to the mainstream" as Betzinez was, through education, rather than through capture and imprisonment as Geronimo was. Eastman was just four years old in 1862 when the Santee took part in the great Sioux uprising and massacre in what is now called Minnesota. Eastman's father was captured and sentenced to death, but Eastman's mother and others in the family fled into Canada where Eastman was raised to age sixteen in the old ways, expecting some day to return to the United States to take revenge for the father who, he thought, had been hanged. But his father's sentence had been commuted to life in prison, where he was converted to Christianity, decided to take the white man's road, learned farming, won release on parole, and finally went to Canada looking for his son. One day, wearing white man's clothes, he walked into the Santee village where his nearly grown son was living, and presently walked out again, taking his son back to the United States. The son, given the name Charles Eastman, was put into mission school, then Beloit College, Knox College, and Dartmouth. Graduating with honors in 1887, he went to medical school at Boston University, where he got his M.D. just in time to be sent out to the Pine Ridge Sioux Agency shortly before the 1890 massacre of Sioux by the Seventh Cavalry at Wounded Knee. Eastman writes of trying to save some of the Indian children wounded there by the Hotchkiss machine guns, or the more prosaic carbines used by the troopers as they followed and shot down the women and children trying to flee the slaughter.

Such are the facts. I want to look, however, not at the Cavalry versus Redskins scenario so familiar from movies, but at one aspect of Eastman's *education as a "wild" Indian*, before being *civilized*. That aspect, briefly examined in the previous chapter, is his learning the Santee system of names for animals and plants, and how this system tied his sense of personal identity to his sense of tribal identity and relationship to the world of other-than-human "natural" beings. In his chapter on "An Indian Boy's Training" (pp. 49–56),

Eastman points out that the education of Indian children was highly systematic and its customs "scrupulously adhered to and transmitted from one generation to another." While a male child was being carried in its mother's womb, she would keep in mind for him some celebrated figure from the tribe's history and "would gather from tradition all his noted deeds and daring exploits, rehearsing them to herself when alone." After he was born, her lullabies would "speak of wonderful exploits in hunting and in war," and he would be called "the future defender of his people." As he grew older, he would be hearing the hunting songs, and in these, "the leading animals are introduced; they come to the boy to offer their bodies for the sustenance of his tribe. The animals are regarded as his friends and spoken of almost as tribes of people or as his cousins, grandfathers, and grandmothers." What Eastman's account here barely hints when the animals are said to "offer their bodies"[15] may well be what is made explicit in the ceremonies of a related tribe, the Osage, particularly in the *Origin Wi-gi-e of the Buffalo Bull Clan* that might be recited as part of the feast of corn given a year after a child was named.[16] In this recitation, a member of the *Tho-xe* (Buffalo Bull) clan tells of how the Osages came from the mid-heavens, the stars, to become a people on this earth. In this journey they were directed by various powers through three "divisions" of the heavens, where they found no place to become a people, but in the fourth "division" they met "the Man of Mystery, the god of the clouds" (understood to be "Thunder," though all these terms are much more than "literal").[17] He said to them: "I am a person of whom your little ones may make their bodies. *When they make of me their bodies*, they shall cause themselves to become deathless" [emphasis added]. They then went to the Buffalo Bull, who also said they could make their bodies of him, and proceeded to throw himself upon the ground so that there sprang up for their use as medicine and food certain plants—including four kinds of corn.

What the Osage chants show is that when the "clan" animals came to offer their bodies it was not only (as Eastman's printed account seems to say) as willing sacrifices for food and clothing and ceremonial regalia—it was as part of the sacred agreement made at Origin

Time between human and non-human beings of this world, between Osage beings on the one hand, and on the other hand beings from Thunder through Mountain Lion and Red Bird "down" (or "up") to the stones of the earth. I believe Eastman's account should be taken as implying that among the Santee the same was true, that when Eastman heard the "hunting songs" he would hear them as part of the Creation Stories and the Origin Stories and the Naming Stories.

Eastman's account does describe what I take to be the telling of Santee creation stories—the "legends of his ancestors and his race" were told and repeated "almost every evening," and whatever story a boy heard one night from parents or grandparents, he himself was "usually required to repeat" the next evening. In this way "his household became the audience by which he was alternately criticized and applauded." It was a schooling without having home and school separated, without creating a clerical class within the tribe.

But what interests me here is the naming system. Let's consider once more Eastman's description of how his uncle "catechized" him on his observation of animals: "It was his custom to let me name all the new birds that I had seen during the day. I would name them according to the color or the shape of the bill or their song or the appearance and locality of the nest—in fact, anything about the bird that impressed me as characteristic. . . . He then usually informed me of the correct name. Occasionally I made a hit and this he would warmly commend." Part of Eastman's Santee identity-sense came from realizing that his own close observation of the birds, and his naming them based on this, might well be at one with his community's choice of names for them. He was adjusting his own verbal creativity to his tribesmen's traditions in a very direct way. The sense of linguistic "authority" in his "oral" society seems just as strong as it is in our "literate" society, but the whole relation of individual to authority must have had a different "feel" in the oral society, where spoken language came from authorities present and known. English speakers have two sets of names for creatures— "common" and "scientific," and in neither set is it apparent to an ordinary speaker *why* a given name is used for a given creature. Our word-roots are buried far out of mind in unknown history.[18] But for

Eastman, his language was "transparent," not "opaque" as English is to most of us. English is a melting-pot language, with a priestly language of Latinate terms, and a commoners' language of shorter words, but all of them are opaque so far as animals are concerned.[19] Our words no longer put us in touch with the LAND we live on and from, or the ANIMALS we live among and upon.

So far, we have focused on three autobiographies only—those of Geronimo, Betzinez, and Eastman. We have posited a "wild" sense of identity with its hierarchy from cosmic to personal firmly set, and a "tame" sense dependent on white beneficence and cultural power; and we have touched briefly on how the "wild" sense (as in Eastman) may have been shaped by the language as used by its speakers. Let's look now at two other tribes, Pawnee and Osage, to observe in more detail how the *land-orientation* of a family and individual created an Indian identity among Pawnees, and how the *naming ceremony* (for persons) helped create Indian identity among Osages. We turn to these two distinctly different tribes because they show it is *Indian* and not just an *Apache* or *Santee* "identity" we are looking at. The sample, admittedly, is limited, but it seems to me cautious inferences can be drawn from it.

For the Pawnees we draw mostly upon Gene Weltfish's beautiful book, *The Lost Universe.*[20] Our point is how powerful a force the Pawnee ceremonies were in shaping each Pawnee's sense of identity. Weltfish says: "The thing that made life most worthwhile to the Pawnees was their elaborate round of ceremonies . . . based on a complex philosophy of the creation of the universe and of man and of their ongoing nature. The ceremonies were considered as the means for keeping the cosmic order in its course and the continuance of the earth and its life processes. . . . . The ceremonies were more than religious observances. They were the whole focus of Pawnee aesthetic life" (p. 8). Nor were these "ceremonial ways" only dances and songs and recitations. The shape of a Pawnee house, and the place in this house of each inhabitant, were part of an ordered patterning that placed this person in a certain clear relation to kinfolk, to household tasks, to the working areas and the sacred areas— *and to the cosmos.* That is, the circular Pawnee lodge was oriented not just within the village, but within the universe, by the sun and stars:

> Everyone in the house knew his appointed place and where he could go
> and . . . not go. In the sacred area at the west was an earthen platform.
> . . . . Between the fireplace and the buffalo altar, there was a sacred spot
> that was invisible—the *wi-haru*, "the place where the wise words of
> those who have gone before us are resting." Rather than step over this
> place in order to pass from one side of the house to the other, every-
> one walked around the entire house by the way of the east. When the
> heads of the household sat down . . . it was to the west . . . and no one
> would want to pass in front of them. The house was a microcosm of the
> universe and as one was at home inside, one was also at home in the
> outside world. For the dome of the sky was the . . . roof of the universe
> and the horizon . . . was the circular wall of the cosmic house. Through
> the roof . . . the star gods poured down their strength from their ap-
> propriate directions in a constant stream. In the west was the Evening
> Star, . . . and in her garden the corn and buffalo were constantly being
> renewed . . . and in the western part of the house the sacred buffalo
> skull and the bundle with its ears of corn symbolized this power. In
> the eastern sky was the Morning Star—god of light, of fire, and of war.
> As he rose every morning he sent his beam into the long entryway of
> the house and lit the fire in an act of cosmic procreation, symbolizing
> his first union with the Evening Star in the times of the great creation
> [when they begot] the girl that was the first human being. . . . The
> house was also the womb of a woman, and the household activities
> represented her reproductive powers. The beds of the women along the
> circular walls were . . . ranged by age to represent the main stages in
> a woman's life—the youngest woman near the west where the garden
> of the Evening Star was located, the mature woman in the middle . . .
> and the old women near the exit to the east, for at their age they were
> "on the way out." Being at home was spoken of as being "inside"; *ti-ka,*
> "he-is-inside"; the house, *a-ka-ru,* "the-inside-place"; the universe, *ka-*
> *huraru,* "the-inside-land." . . . Everyone in the house had a clear con-
> sciousness of these things as they moved about within it. Now secure
> in his bed, the boy was also secure in the world. (pp. 63–64)

Naturally, to be oriented to heaven and the stars meant one was oriented in time as well as space, among the seasons and the cere-

monies that "marked" the seasons: except that for a Pawnee, a ceremony did not merely mark, it helped in the moving of time.[21] There
was, for instance, the "spring awakening": "The first ceremonial act
of the year was to awaken the whole earth from its winter sleep. . . .
The year began about the time of the spring equinox with the ritual
recitation of the creation by the five priests. The position of the stars
was an important guide to the time. . . . The earth lodge served as an
astronomical observatory and as the priests sat inside at the west,
they could observe the stars in certain positions through the smoke-
hole and through the long east-oriented entranceway" (p. 12). Each
Pawnee therefore knew from the repeated ceremonies how the Creation began, and saw the ordering of that creation symbolized in the
shape and orientation of the house and its inhabitants, saw the seasonal occupations and activities closely tied to the stars, observed
that the singing and dancing ceremonies were part of the link between self and tribe and universe, part of a Pawnee being.

From these facts I would argue that the "wild" Indian held quite
different opinions from "civilized" Americans around 1880, concern-
ing a person's relation to land, sky, and the creatures therewithin.
They differed not only in their notions about property and owner-
ship, or in their political views on voting, taxation, churchgoing,
salvation and damnation. Geronimo, in being Apache, was like a
Pawnee, or a Santee, or an Omaha, or an Osage: all were *Indian*,
not *Euroamerican*. I suggest that for all the anthropologists can say
about differences of high importance between cultures of Plains,
Pueblo, Woodlands, Coastal and other tribes, groups, nations, there
WAS such a thing as an "Indian" way beneath the differences. Succinctly put, that way's ceremonies *embodied a unified way of life:*
what was Indian was the seamlessness of human life, in which it
would not make sense to speak of religion on the one hand, and warfare on the other, of hunting here and naming a new chief there, of
the Creation of the Universe on this side and the Naming of a Child
on that. "History" and "village arrangement," "Cosmos" and "lodge
architecture," were intimately related through ceremonies as well
as stories and art work; the inside of a lodge, as well as placement of
houses in the camp, carried historic and cosmic meanings.

The best way to demonstrate this might be a detailed discussion of ways in which, for instance, the Osage ceremonies for naming a child reflect, are linked with, those for naming a new chief, and both ceremonial cycles embody the tribe's history as well as its Genesis-Exodus version. Having discussed the Osage Naming Ceremony at length elsewhere, I will focus here on a few points from Francis La Flesche's account. Himself Omaha and speaking Osage well, La Flesche was the right person at the right time to preserve in print Osage ceremonies that would shortly afterwards be "thrown away." In the Osage *Rite of the Chiefs*, as he notes, are not only the ceremonies for naming a new chief, but (in what we may call allegorical narrative form) the history of the Osage people's becoming a nation. We are told in this rite how they came from the stars and chose bodily forms, how they took the tribal organization that simultaneously represented their history and the form of the universe. In the ceremony one finds, also, explanation of the choosing of certain animals as patrons for their clans, certain foods as the right ones, certain names for individuals as appropriate (and as tied to their mythic and in-time history). In this *Rite of the Chiefs*, therefore, what Europeans would subdivide into "history, religion, social structure, farming, hunting and ethology" are all subsumed. This rite was supplemented by another which La Flesche titles *Hearing of the Sayings of the Ancient Men*, in which we also see expressed "in mythical form, the origin of the people," here envisioned as a begetting of life between "two great fructifying forces—namely the sky and the earth," with life continuing forever to proceed from this begetting. And this notion of a continuous procreating of the universe is embodied in the tribal organization, divided into moieties of Sky and Earth divisions, with men from one of these required to marry women from the other, so that for each Osage marriage arrangement and ceremony there was a reenactment of the tribe's origins and of the cosmic reasons and theory behind this.[22] Further, the version of this origin-story recited by a given clan was modified so as to "conform to that part of nature which the [clan] represented in the tribal and the gentile organizations, for the tribe in its entirety symbolized the visible universe in all its known aspects." Specifically, the Black Bear or Thunder clan would each have its own version, with its particular patron-being giving its special name, powers, and blessing to the clan and the tribe.

Such, then, were the *Rite of the Chiefs* and the *Hearing of the Sayings of the Ancient Men*. When we now look at the Osage rite for naming a child—which as La Flesche puts it "installs the child in his proper place in the tribal organization and entitles him to recognition as a person"—we do not see an isolated and unrelated set of stories and histories. We find instead that the names bestowed in the bringing of a child into a clan reflect the tribal and gentile histories. The name *Nom-peh-wah-the*, for instance, may be literally translated as "Fear-Inspiring," but that is only the surface part of its meaning. Literally, *nom-peh* means "to be afraid," and *wah-the* means "cause or make to be." But the fear referred to in this name, it is understood, is that caused by Thunder: the sacred Thunder of the time before the Osages came to earth, when they sent ahead a messenger to discover how they might become a people, and what they could make their bodies from and what names they might take. The name *Nom-peh-wah-the* therefore embodies and recalls this part of the people's sacred history, as well as that part of its chronicle-history when certain famous men bore this name in the memory of the elders.[23]

Clearly, then, giving a clan-name involved a ceremony that itself was an epicycle on the great cycle of clan-origin, which was part of the universe's wheel that had turned to bring the entire tribe and its world into being. The Osages, we may stress, believed that the universe did move in an order given it by a "silent, invisible creative power . . . named *Wa-kon-dah*, Mysterious Power."[24] Therefore, when the first ceremony in the child-naming ritual was called *Wa-zho-i-ga-the*, "the Taking of Bodies," it was not merely that some incorporeal star-beings decided to come down and incarnate themselves, but that they were moving as part of the universe under Wa-kon-dah's guidance. When they adopted their life-symbols through which they became a people and could live on earth, they addressed these as "grandfather" and "grandmother": Sun, Moon, Morning Star, Evening Star, Dipper, Pleiades, Elk, Bear, Puma, Red Cedar, Buffalo Bull. When (at a later stage of the child-naming) the naming *wi-gi-e* of a clan was recited, the recital was called the *Zha-zhe Ki-ton*, "Taking of Names." The names were given according to a set sequence of possibilities determined in part by the order of birth within a family: first male, second male, third male; first, second, third female—each had its possible set of names.[25]

At the ceremony's end, there would be a special set of instructions for the child's mother. At the later feast (including corn ceremonially planted by the mother) for the *Xo-ka* who had presided over the naming, there might be the recitation by a member of the Buffalo Bull clan of that clan's *wi-gi-e,* telling how the Osages descended from the heavens and—most pertinently—how the Buffalo Bull had brought corn to the Osages. And to recur to the name just mentioned, *Nom-peh-wah-the,* this *wi-gi-e* tells how, when the Osages were trying to come down from stars to earth, their messenger was sent ahead to find a place where they might become a people. Having passed through three divisions of the heavens, the messenger had found no habitation for them, but in the Fourth Division he saw the "Man of Mystery, the god of the clouds"—and turning to his brothers, he said: "Here stands a *fear-inspiring man!* His name, I verily believe, is *Nom-peh-wah-the* ("fear-inspiring")!" Thereupon this mysterious and terrible man addresses the messenger and other Osages: "I am a person of whom your little ones may make their bodies. When they make of me their bodies, they shall cause themselves to be deathless."[26] He then gives them other personal names that they can use.

The name *Nom-peh-wah-the,* then, would be given in a context which would bring its new bearer into the tribe in a very complete fashion, at least as complete as a Christian or Jewish naming ceremony—and on its religious and cosmic side it would be comparable to such rites. It also referenced the tribal, family, and clan history into which the newly named child would be precisely placed. An Osage child in those "wild" times would thus have had all these placements brought to his awareness not only at the particular time he was given the name, but each time he attended another name-giving, and also when he attended the *Rites of the Chiefs* and other ceremonies.

In short, like Geronimo, or Eastman, or La Flesche, or a Pawnee child, an Osage would have had his personal identity carefully, explicitly, unmistakably linked with that of his people, with the symbolic arrangement of his village, with the marriage arrangements and hunting encampments and choosing of chiefs and war and peace ceremonies, with the animals whom he could hunt or whose feathers he could wear, the plants he would eat, the earth and sky he dwelt within. If we wanted to ask about a "wild" Indian's sense of identity, therefore, we ought to ask also about these "other" matters. The "wild" Indian was tied to land, people, origins and way of life, by every kind of human order we can imagine. "History" and "Myth" and "Identity" are not three separate matters, here, but three aspects of one human being.

How Columbus Fell from the Sky and Lighted Up Two Continents

Columbus, Milton, Shakespeare,

and the Osage and Navajo Creation Stories

Sublime achievement against great odds, sordid crimes against humanity: reading the logbooks and letters of Christopher Columbus, we meet both these facts. Columbus boldly went where no European before him had gone, and he led a small band of often-frightened and discouraged men with daring and determination beyond what most of us could even imagine. The course of human history was changed by his voyage—made better in many ways for the descendants of Europeans, made far worse in other ways for descendants of Native Americans, in the five hundred years since his glorious and dreadful landing among the gentle unknown people whom the Spaniards would so quickly enslave and slaughter.

Nothing can change what has happened,[1] but history is what we make of what happened, and that means trying to see not just how we came to be where we are, but also where we seem to be headed. We all expect, or so I believe, that our grandchildren or great-grandchildren will steer great starships out toward worlds even more strange and magnificent than the first Paradisal islands where Columbus, looking for an old world, first encountered what seemed to Europeans a new world.

We may all be very wrong: the little green beings in their huge and powerful ships may land on our shores, our science prove too weak for their divine powers, we earthly beings may be enslaved, tortured, exterminated in our turn. Perhaps it is worthwhile, therefore, to set down here a few thoughts about the Columbian encounter, as a way to look at future encounters—whether they happen during some glorious voyage out among other stars, or precede a sudden holocaust of humans on the Paradisal world we now inhabit, or lead to assimilation with the little green beings if they should be less murderous than the Europeans proved to be. Wherever we are headed, then, here is a re-view of that Columbian encounter. It juxtaposes words from Columbus, Milton, and Shakespeare, and draws less familiar parallels—and contrasts—between Columbian, Navajo, and Osage versions of how and why we, and our nations, have come to be what we are, where we are, and who we are.

Paradise Found and *Paradise Lost*

Columbus, in his letter on this first voyage, reports that the people who came to meet him, as he landed, "have no religion and are not idolaters; but all believe that power and goodness dwell in the sky and they are firmly convinced that I have come from the sky."[2] Reading this, I could not help recalling the great lines from *Paradise Lost* where Milton retells the Roman myth of Vulcan, god of fire and technology: Vulcan, who had angered Jupiter, was thrown out of Heaven and brought his craft to humans, much as Columbus brought it to the "New World." Milton expected his readers to remember that the Roman gods were devils in disguise: Vulcan took the appearance of a god to seduce humans away from the worship of the true God.

Milton gave the devil his due—some of the most magnificent lines in *Paradise Lost*. He fingers Vulcan as the architect of Hell's Palace of Pandemonium (a word Milton coined to mean "city of all the Demons"), and pictures the fallen angels, now devils, as awed when they first enter. This brilliant technologist, this urban architect Vulcan (Milton tells us), had earlier designed the high-rises of Heaven,

and we feel in the rhythm and cadences of Milton's lines all that
had been lost in such a being's corruption and fall:

> His [Vulcan's] hand was known
> In Heaven by many a towered structure high,
> Where sceptred angels held their residence
> And sat as princes, whom the Supreme King
> Exalted to such power, and gave to rule,
> Each in his hierarchy, the orders bright.
> Nor was his name unheard or unadored
> In ancient Greece; and in Ausonian land [Italy]
> Men called him Mulciber, and how he fell
> From Heaven they fabled, thrown by angry Jove
> Sheer o'er the crystal battlements: from morn
> Till noon he fell, from noon to dewy eve,
> A summer's day, and with the setting sun
> Dropped from the zenith like a falling star
> On Lemnos, the Aegean isle. Thus they relate,
> Erring—for he with this rebellious rout
> Fell long before.[3]

Reading those lines, I remember that Columbus served the absolute monarchs of Spain, with all its romantic castles and cathedrals
("towered structures high"), and its Grand Inquisitor. He brought
to the people of this hemisphere a technology and a palace-making
power almost as great as (in Milton's account) Vulcan had brought
first to Hell and then to Europe—and I think Columbus carried, in
his Niña, Pinta, and Santa Maria, along with noble plans for a heavenly city, the ignoble politics of Pandemonium.

Columbus himself pictures the "new world" he had "discovered"
as very like the oldest world of which he knew: Eden and its Garden
of Paradise. He records in the logbook of his first voyage, on Sunday 21 October, what he saw as he stepped ashore on the island he
would name, for the Queen of Spain, *Isabela:*

The trees and plants are as green as in Andalusia in April. The singing of small birds is so sweet that no one could ever wish to leave this

place. Flocks of parrots darken the sun and there is a marvelous variety of large and small birds very different from our own; the trees are of many kinds, each with its own fruit, and all have a marvelous scent. It grieves me extremely that I cannot identify them, for I am quite certain that they are all valuable and I am bringing samples of them and of the plants also. As I was walking beside one of the lagoons I saw a snake, which we killed. I am bringing it to your highness.[4]

You see (Columbus marvels), I stepped from *October* onto an island, and found myself in *April's* blossoms and birdsong! Moreover, as he notes elsewhere for his Christian readers (for whom it would be a sign of the Earthly Paradise), flower, leaf, and fruit here grow all at once on the same trees, not dying the seasonal death which Adam's fall had brought into the world as Europeans know it.

It is remarkable that Columbus noted the serpent's presence, that he killed it, and yet that he did not read any Christian symbolism into this. The island might resemble Eden, but Columbus was not about to suggest that he would let it remain unfallen. In fact, he was already planning how to take over this paradise, enslave its gentle inhabitants, and convert its fruitful innocents into wealth for Spain's monarchs, and a dukedom for himself and his heirs: "Should your highnesses command it all the inhabitants could be taken away to Castile or held as slaves on the island, for with fifty men we could subjugate them all and make them do what we wish. . . . Generally it was my wish to pass no island without taking possession of it, though having annexed one it might be said that we had annexed all."[5] He carefully notes every instance of a gold ornament on any of the natives, remarks that they *do not prize it as riches but only for its ornamental value*, observes that they are extremely generous and trusting (in these first encounters; the natives before very long saw that trust was hardly the right attitude if they wanted to keep their lives and freedom), and he sends men to search for gold at every opportunity. During his second voyage (1493–96), as his son Hernando tells us, Columbus concluded that the natives had no concept of private property: "On entering these houses, the Indians whom the Admiral brought from Isabela promptly seized anything that pleased them and the owners showed no sign of resentment. *They seemed to hold all possessions in common* [emphasis mine]. They took from him whatever they liked, in the belief that similar customs obtained among us. But they were quickly undeceived."[6]

Columbus had remarked, in the letter on his first voyage, on the sexual arrangements, private property, and distribution of food among the natives: "The men are seemingly content with one woman, but their chief or king is allowed more than twenty. The women appear to work more than the men and I have not been able to find out if they have private property. As far as I could see whatever a man had was shared among all the rest and this particularly applies to food."[7] In other words, Columbus did not notice any instances of people going hungry while others had plenty or more than enough. There were no homeless, there were no hungry, there were no poor when he arrived, so far as he could see.

It would be naive to claim that the actual condition of all the natives was so Edenic as the passages quoted above seem meant to suggest. Columbus, like all the later explorers, had to raise funds for exploring, and therefore had to be a master of public relations and hype—as we see in his log, his letters, and his son's account of his voyages, where Columbus keeps assuring readers that there are fantastic amounts of gold on the very next island, which he has not yet managed to explore. His praise of the unbelievable fertility apparent in the lush growth of useful and delicious plants, his harping on the docility of the natives, were meant to help win further funding, so as to recruit more soldiers, laborers, craftsmen, and clergy to turn this Eden into a Christian empire, with himself as its viceroy.

Cannibals and the "Mirror of All Christian Kings"

So Columbus deliberately gilded the lily he found. But he does show us, growing around that lily, lots of poison ivy. Or—so he claimed, at least—he discovered that there were cannibals on some islands, and some definitely "fallen" behavior: raiding, abduction, castration, rape, looting. If reading Columbus sometimes reminds me of reading Milton, at other times some of his firsthand descriptions of behavior among the natives of this "New World" remind me of scenes from Shakespeare. About the Caribs, for instance, the physician named Dr. Chanca (whom Ferdinand and Isabela sent with Columbus on his second voyage) wrote, "These people raid the other islands and carry off all the women they can take, especially the young and beautiful, whom they keep as servants and concubines. . . . These women say that they are treated with a cruelty that seems incredible. The Caribs eat the male children that they have by them. . . . They castrate the boys that they capture and use them as servants until they are men. Then they kill and eat them."[8] There are serious doubts about these reports, documented in, for instance, Kirkpatrick Sale's discussion of them in *The Conquest of Paradise.* Sale suggests that Europeans projected upon these island peoples the old myths of the Anthropophagi, demonizing the newly discovered humans in order to justify enslaving or exterminating them. He also points out that cannibalism was a practice "by no means unknown in Europe itself."[9] But assuming for argument's sake that the Caribs did practice some sort of cannibalism, we would certainly say, as Dr. Chanca did: "The customs of these Carib people are beastly." And yet, his words remind me of a passage in Shakespeare's *Henry the Fifth,* in which King Henry warns the French citizens of the town of Harfleur, which he is besieging, of what will happen to them if they continue to resist his siege. (The incident dates historically from 1415, during the Hundred Years' War between England and France over who should be king of France.) Shakespeare presents King Henry as the "mirror of all Christian kings," a very interesting view since in the third act of the play Henry tells the mayor of Harfleur that if the town surrenders its inhabitants will be treated leniently, but if they have to be defeated by siege then the victorious English soldiers will behave very much like the Caribs whom Dr. Chanca found so beastly:

> For as I am a soldier,
> A name that in my thoughts becomes me best,
> If I begin the battery once again,
>
> . . . .
>
> The gates of mercy shall be all shut up,
> And the fleshed soldier, rough and hard of heart,

In liberty of bloody hand shall range
With conscience wide as hell, mowing like grass
Your fresh fair virgins and your flowering infants.
  . . . .
What is it to me, if you yourselves are cause,
If your pure maidens fall into the hand
Of hot and forcing violation?
  . . . .
Take pity on your town and of your people,
Whiles yet my soldiers are in my command—
  . . . .
If not, why, in a moment look to see
The blind and bloody soldier with foul hand
Defile the locks of your shrill-shrieking daughters,
Your fathers taken by their silver beards
And their most reverend heads dashed to the walls;
Your naked infants spitted upon pikes,
While the mad mothers with their howls confused
Do break the clouds, as did the wives of Jewry
At Herod's bloody-hunting slaughtermen.
What say you? Will you yield, and this avoid?
Or *guilty in defence* [emphasis mine], be thus destroyed?[10]

It is clear to anyone reading Dr. Chanca's unverified account of how the Caribs raided, murdered, raped, looted, and kidnapped that their acts match fairly closely—except for the accusation of cannibalism, which is perhaps a European slander—the description given by King Henry of what his soldiers will just "naturally" do, if the mayor of Harfleur should try to defend his town against Henry's invading army. King Henry, it may be said, is invading only to validate his claim that he is the true King of France, a claim Shakespeare had carefully assigned to be validated for Henry by the Archbishop of Canterbury in a long earlier speech in the play; and Henry's words succinctly state the standard Renaissance theory of warfare, that where a besieged city has been breached but continues to resist and thus to cost the lives of besieging soldiers, the besiegers can legitimately take any vengeance they please (as payment, more or less) for the unnecessary loss of lives. However, the mayor of Harfleur knows that if he should accept Henry's claims and surrender without a fight, and then the reigning French king should kick Henry out, the French king could behead the mayor as a traitor for surrendering the city. The rules of European warfare were very orderly but not very pleasant for those in the mayor's position. The powerful can do anything and justify it, but the weak had better do whatever the most powerful say, or they will be destroyed. If the weak wait to see who *is* most powerful, as the mayor is trying to do, they can "legitimately" be beheaded (and worse!) for waiting.

Surely the "gentle" Tainos, caught between the crossbows of Columbus and the clubs of their rivals the Caribs, would have recognized in that besieged mayor of Harfleur and his citizens their fellow hostages to threatening "savage" powers. Surely, too, they would have understood that when Dr. Chanca exclaimed that the Carib customs were *beastly*, the good Doctor was looking into a mirror— or, as Shakespeare put it, at *the mirror of all Christian kings.*

In the Fast Track of the Columbus 500

The usual next step in an essay on Columbus would be to turn from old negative to new positive. After all, I sit typing this on a laptop, the splendid product of a European technology (or, in the decades of NAFTA and GATT, with jobs handed over by transnational corporations to the lowest-paid laborers, is it an Asiatic or a Multinational Corporation technology?)—despite my having just compared the introducer of such skills to a devil who was once hurled from heaven after inventing gunpowder. And I live comfortably in a green suburb, two streets from the serenely expensive university where I have tenure. I write in the English language, mind-crafted over thousands of years and given to me at birth, at ease in the most powerful and one of the freest nations of the earth. The shapers of this nation— heirs of Columbus—worked to make better living conditions, both material and spiritual, than were possible in the "old" Europe. All this, as an American citizen, I acknowledge is true.

And in the One-Eyed Ford[11]

Yet within this bountiful nation, millions of humans are less well cared for than were the island natives where Columbus first landed. Homeless and hungry people cannot get good medical care because they have no money, insurance, status. People barely one rung above homeless are being loansharked legally by the interest rates on credit cards dealt out to them, like losing hands in a poker game, by slick bankers holding the pot. We live in a good society—but good mostly for those with "good" educations, the right skin color, friends, banks.

Nor is it only humans who suffer more in this our great nation than did the natives in their small islands. Our relatives also ache: animals and plants, the air, the water, earth herself. The electricity that brilliantly lights New York City is not generated on Manhattan itself: rather, out in "the sticks," sulfurous fires send their acid and cinders up into the lungs and flowers of every living creature downwind from "towered structures high." From this burning and pollution, set on the green prairie or in dusty desert, comes the power that lights our thousand-storied New York, Los Angeles, Las Vegas—our neon jungles, our family rooms. If a Phoenix glitters and bathes itself in snowmelt waters there in Arizona, we can see from our jet planes the fouled nest it sprang from, the smoke and scars of Black Mesa coalpits in the Navajo Nation: the price paid by Navajo, Hopi, and all of us, for our "enlightenment."

We also tap other veins for this god-juice, our fix of electrons that seem to alter time and space by spilling the long-dead music of Beethoven, or far-off wars from other continents, or from this one, into our living rooms. From infinitesimal atomic nuclei we suck the power we need, then spit out the glowing ash it leaves, bury it deep in the future for grandchildren to step upon—though sun and wind and water wait like angels for us to turn their power into a light that would leave less ash, less oily smoke, than the flames of Kuwait, fewer oil-fouled shores and sea creatures than the tankers of Exxon, less leukemia and abortion than the eruptions of Chernobyl.

Put simply, we still have not bettered what Columbus found when he stepped ashore to meet those who had cared for this continent

until then. If and when I see a United States where the hungry all
are fed, where differences in ability, income, and race are not used
to divide us into a wealthy and overfed few on the one hand, and a
hungry, ill-fed, ill-housed many on the other, *then* I will agree that
the coming of Columbus was not a bad thing. And if I see Indian
nations free and healthy again, I'll be happy to celebrate!

How the Osage Nation Came from the Sky

But we have focused thus far on Columbus and what the Europeans
have made of this continent, making only brief mention of how well
the Indians seem to have managed *before* Columbus got here. It
might be thought that such management was "just natural," that the
Indians had no consciousness of ordering themselves or achieving
harmony with the world they lived in. Let us, then, compare Adam's
apple with Montezuma's papaya, so to speak: let us see how two pre-
Columbian societies conceived and dedicated themselves (as Lincoln phrased it) to the proposition that all men are created equal—
and to the nobler proposition that all beings are our equals. These
matters are dealt with in the Creation Stories—those parts of sacred
tribal histories that tell how Osages came to be Osage, Navajos to be
Navajo, in this very world, among its very creatures and conditions.

During the Osage Naming Ceremony, for instance, each of the
tribal clan-representatives present would recite that clan's version
of the Osage Creation Story, as a way of affirming that the child
being named was descended from those first beings who came into
this world as founders of the Osage Nation. These beings, in the
Osage story, came from the stars, at a time after this world had been
created as the Waters, and the Earth, and the Sky. At that time, those
who would become the Osage Nation decided to come to this world.
Being sensible and cautious people, they sent ahead many scouts to
find out how they might live and become an enduring people in the
world as it had been created and shaped. Each of the scouts traveled
ahead, and each met a sacred being who offered help in finding the
right ways to live in this world. These sacred beings included the

Eagle, the Red Cedar, the Buffalo, Elk, Black Bear, and others; each
of these then became the guide for a "clan" or *gens* of the Osage
Nation. In each meeting, the sacred being said the same thing: *If
you make your bodies of me, you will live to see old age, and live
into the peaceful days.*

The Osages saw human and "animal" relations differently from
the way these are viewed in the biblical accounts, which Columbus
would have known. In the Bible, Adam and Eve are in one version created together in God's image; in another, Eve is made from
Adam's rib, after the animals have been created.[12] The animals are
not only subordinate, but subservient, to humans. In contrast, the
Osages tell of meeting the animals of this world in a sacred dimension, before actually descending into this world—and they are given,
by the animals, the wisdom to live here in a good way that will
allow them to endure into "the peaceful days," a ritual term which
implies more than just "old age."

The Osage account has profound wisdom. As our "animal scientists" continue to discover, animals *do* show us how to live in this
world. They came into this world long before we did and, as we
are discovering, some of their ways of sensing its phenomena, of
finding their way around among its powers and dangers, anticipate
and rival our high-tech devices and procedures. If, for instance, we
ask how Columbus managed to sail across the Atlantic Ocean, we
know that he had a magnetic compass, something fairly new in
navigational technology, recorded from European sources of the late
twelfth century A.D., perhaps used in the East about that time also,
according to encyclopedias. He steered by the sun and stars, but
when they were not visible, he could steer by his compass. We are
just beginning to understand a little of how animals map their world
and what they use to navigate within it: in the June 1991 *National
Geographic*, for instance, I read that pigeons "see ultraviolet light
and hear extremely low-frequency sound. . . . From anywhere in
the United States, . . . [their] keen ears hear a volcano erupting
in Java or winds swirling around the Andes."[13] It may be that tiny
specks of ferrite in the pigeon's brain are linked to sensory nerves
and allow it to "see" magnetic lines of force; certainly the ability

to see light-polarization shows it the sun even behind clouds. Our nuclear submarines under the Arctic ice are, perhaps, kept aware of what is going on in Washington or Moscow by the kind of "ultra-low sound" that alerts pigeons to the volcanoes of Java, the surf patterns of California or North Carolina, the thunderstorms of Colorado, the tornadoes on their way to the dovecote.[14] Watch the birds, and forecast the storms of next weekend, or this afternoon? Well, perhaps the Indians were right to respect what animals can teach us.

In the Osage Creation Story, which was recited as part of the Naming Ceremony and therefore was heard many times by assembled families as their children were being "brought into" the tribal society, we see animals as partners, teachers, and helpers, welcoming us into this world, giving us ways to survive and prevail in our earthly lives. Perhaps when the Tainos thought Columbus "came from the sky," and welcomed him to this world that was new to him, they had some such belief in mind: a new group of beings, in those three ships, was coming to this world, and those already here could welcome and show them how to survive.

One more point has always come up, whenever we have discussed the Osage Naming Ceremony in my classes on American Indian literature: is it only "mythmaking" to say that humans come from the stars? Is it more "factually accurate" to say that humans are made out of this earth we live on, as is said in the Hebrew Creation Story? To these questions, I respond with another: where does this earth come from, if not from the stars? Not just ordinary stars either, but from supernovas, in whose explosions are produced all the heavier elements in our human bodies; so if we are formed of the dust of the ground, that dust is also star-stuff. And as for this planet Earth, it is certainly among the stars, is it not? We *do* come "from the stars," just as we *do* come "from the earth." The old Hebrews got it right; so did the old Osages. Thinking about the "old myths" can perhaps have its humbling uses. It may well be that myths are like the stars: we see by their light, even though they may have "died" centuries ago.

How the Navajo Nation Came from the Earth

The Osages are hardly the only Indian nation to build such wisdom into their stories. Consider, for instance, the Navajo Creation Story, and particularly three points which "mainstream" readers might ponder. First is the way the Navajo storytellers have evidently added to their earlier "Gambler" stories one that deals with the Europeans who had by then conquered Mexico; in this we see how flexible the Navajo "canon" of sacred stories could be, allowing them to present and comment on the "new" people of the continent. A second point is what the Navajo can tell us about sexual relations. And a third is a caution we need to consider when we think of eliminating evils from our world. (In discussing these matters, I ask for tolerance from the Navajo people; my knowledge of Navajo ways is very limited, and the following remarks rely mostly on Paul Zolbrod's *Diné Bahanè, The Navajo Creation Story.*)[15]

Why the Gambler Was Sent to Mexico

The powerful Gambler first appears well into the Navajo Creation Story, after the people have come up from the First World through the Second, Third, and Fourth into the Fifth World in which we live. At that time, "a gambling god" descends into the midst of the Pueblo people and challenges them to "all sorts of games," which he always wins (*DB*, p. 99). He soon has won all the possessions of the Pueblo villagers, forces them to build a racetrack and an arena for his gambling games, and reduces them all to slave laborers.

Until then, the ancestors of the Navajo had remained aloof from this disaster, tending their own affairs. But one day, the kindly Talking God comes to them and tells a young Navajo man that the Gambler has just won the shells which are the greatest treasures of the Pueblo peoples, kept by them for the Sun, and the Gambler refuses to return these treasures to the Sun. Now the Sun and other Holy People are going to assemble in the mountains and decide what to do about this Gambler. The young Navajo man is invited to attend and there finds that the animals who are pets of the Pueblo people, but whom the Gambler now "owns," have come to the meeting, "unhappy at being someone else's property."

The Navajo conspires with the gods and animals to outwit the Gambler. With the young Navajo fronting for them, and using in turn the powers of the various gods and animals, they win everything back from the Gambler. When he curses gods and humans, they tell him: "Remember that you bet your very self, and admit that you have lost. . . . You are not one of the Holy People. . . . You may have gained power over some of your own kind. But you have no such power over us. Not here in this world" (DB, p. 110). At this, the god Wind draws a magic bow, places the Gambler in it like an arrow, and shoots him into the sky, the realm of the mischief-making god Begochidi. When the Gambler tells his sad story to this god, he gets sympathy—so much, that Begochidi decides to make the Gambler rich and powerful once again.

Here is where we see the Navajo have added to their original Creation Story's section on the Gambler an episode that deals with the post-Columbus situation. In this addition, Begochidi makes the Gambler rich again by creating for him a whole new people, the Mexicans, as well as the domestic animals brought to America by the Europeans: sheep, burros, pigs, goats, and horses. Begochidi then sends the Gambler and these newly created beings back into our Fifth World—not to Pueblo and Navajo country, this time, but to "a place far to the south," Mexico: "Having died there soon after his return, he dwells there to this very day as a god of . . . the Mexican people" (DB, p. 112).

Two things strike me about this Gambler episode. One is its socio-economic point, that *it is possible, but socially destructive, for one person to amass great wealth and enslave other people—and that this should be stopped by communal action.* Second is that this point *is carefully turned to apply sharply to Europeans,* since the Gambler is not destroyed (in the post-Columbus version), but is sent back to be the God of the European-created country of Mexico. The Navajo thinkers, it seems, decided that while the robber-baron mentality is a bad thing among Pueblo and Navajo people, it is well suited to the European colonial society. Not only, then, has the

Navajo Creation Story been adapted at this point to take account of the coming of the Europeans, it offers a shrewd and realistic comment on the social values and dynamics of those Europeans. It identifies, if we want to draw a New Testament parallel, Mammon as a God of the European society, and suggests, just as Jesus did, that it is sometimes reasonable to "make friends with the Mammon of iniquity." I wonder what the Navajo storytellers made of that part of the Christian Gospels?

Making Sex Beautiful—But Not Too Beautiful

So the drive for money and possessions and power was firmly put by the Navajo Creation Story into its proper place. But what about the sexual drives, and social relations between men and women? On these matters, the Navajo account seems much fuller than what Columbus found in his Bible. Adam and Eve were commanded to be fruitful and multiply, but God said little about the proper relations between men and women, in either of the two biblical narratives of how humans were created.[16] After laying down divine policy—to populate the earth—God seems not to have legislated the details, leaving Adam and Eve to implement this policy by free enterprise. Commentators divide on just when they began implementing (some say before, some say after the Fall), but it is clear that they succeeded. On the other hand, alert readers might notice that the biblical text is silent about the inevitable implication that, for a good while, such populating must have been done by incest.

The Navajo narrative, in contrast, is outspoken and detailed. Once First Man and First Woman had been created (the male from a white ear of corn, the female from a yellow one), the gods had a shelter of brushwood made and told them to live together in it as man and wife. Of this union, five pairs of twins were born. The first pair were hermaphrodites, the other four sets each had one male and one female. For a time, the twin pairs lived together as husbands and wives but, growing ashamed of this incest, they found spouses among the Mirage People. First Woman, seeing this change, was glad, but worried that the people would find it too easy to renounce marriage and take new spouses. She thought marriage should be made very attractive, because there is a great deal of work that humans must do and *it is best if they marry and divide the work between them* (DB, p. 53). To ensure that harmony might prevail, marriages should last. Meditating on how to achieve this end, First Woman did not impose negative commandments, nor did she act hastily. Instead, she waited until people had invented farming, irrigating, pottery, farm tools, hunting and hunting ceremonies, and ways to make clothing. Then she acted:

> She fashioned a penis of turquoise. Then she rubbed loose cuticle from a woman's breast and mixed it up with yucca fruit, which she put inside the turquoise penis. . . . Next she made a vagina of white shell. Into the vagina she placed a clitoris of red shell. Then she rubbed loose cuticle from a man's breast and mixed it with yucca fruit, which she placed in the clitoris. And she combined herbs with various kinds of water and placed that mixture deep inside the vagina. That way pregnancy would occur. (DB, p. 55)

> She then not only arranged for both penis and vagina to experience orgasm, she carefully adjusted the intensity of first and second orgasms for each, until she was sure that men and women would learn to care for each other. They would be eager to have children, . . . share the labor evenly, and . . . each more willingly tend to the other's needs. (DB, p. 56)

Even after such thoughtful arrangement, however, things nearly got botched by the intervention of another figure: Coyote, the powerful "trickster" figure. Coyote had come into existence soon after First Woman made the sexual arrangements just described; in fact, he appeared during the puberty ceremonies in which elders were giving a penis to a boy and a vagina to a girl who had come of age. The people at the ceremony noticed that the sky was swooping down to embrace the earth, and just where sky met earth, Coyote and Badger sprang out of the ground (DB, pp. 56–7). Coyote at once came over to watch the puberty ceremony, but in his typical way he decided that he could improve the arrangements, and he proceeded to make the sexual organs a great deal more attractive. First

Woman saw that this "improvement" would cause men and women to be too easily drawn together, so she ordered them to wear clothes whenever in company with other people.

What might Columbus and his men have thought, had they been able to somehow hear and understand this narrative of the way divine powers—with human cooperation, and despite an impish intervention—could integrate the powerful forces of sex and possessive desires into an ordered human society? Would some of those Spanish soldiers have been tempted to think these "Indians" *did* have religion, and powers of social reason, after all? Would they have thought that perhaps this story's account of the "deadly sins" of lust and greed was at least worth comparing with the traditional Christian account of them?

On Slaying Monsters and Disposing of Toxic Waste

Finally, the Navajo Creation Story has a very interesting slant on how to deal with some dangerous by-products of human activities. It seems that despite First Woman's excellent arrangements and good judgment, she and First Man had a fearsome quarrel. First Man had brought deer meat for dinner, but after eating heartily, First Woman belched and thanked her vagina for the delicious meal. First Man, annoyed, asked if she thought her vagina was the great hunter that had brought home this delicious dinner. Why yes, she said—were it not for the vagina, no men would do anything. First Man said, Well! Maybe you women think you can live without us men? The quarrel escalated until First Man just walked out. Next day all the men went over the river, leaving the women to themselves—and all the women said, Good riddance!

At first each group considered that it was doing just fine, and they taunted each other across the river. (One might imagine how this story would later be useful in Navajo domestic situations!) As time went on, however, the needs and difficulties springing from the separation overwhelmed them, and with encouragement from various beings, the men and women got back together. However, a great flood drove them from the Fourth World in which these things had happened, up into the Fifth (our present) World. Even after reaching this safety, dire consequences dogged them, in the form of monsters begotten by sexual self-abuse while the sexes were separated. It was with these monsters that disorder came into the world, and the monsters grew and began to ambush and devour the people, who were reduced to a small number.

At that time, First Man journeyed to the top of Spruce Mountain, and there obtained divine help: the gods brought into existence the powerful figures of Changing Woman and White Shell Woman. Changing Woman then had a son by the Sun, and White Shell Woman had a son by the Water. Grown up, these sons became the Monster Slayers who, by courage, many ruses, and help from Changing Woman and the Sun, destroyed the deadly monsters (DB, pp. 58–78, 94–9, 171–269).

At this point, the Navajo "slant" on how to deal with such evils becomes (to me) most fascinating. When each of the monsters is killed, the Monster-Slaying twins see to it that *something is made of its corpse.* One reason they do this may be hinted at, in the story, when their father the Sun—whose help they need—makes them understand that the monster they are about to kill is the Sun's own child, and therefore is half-brother to the elder of the Monster-Slaying Twins. This implies, surely, that whatever evils human beings have to "wipe out" are likely to be "part of us," instead of being truly "aliens" (DB, p. 211).

How explicit the story is, we can see from an instance or two. When the Twins and the Sun kill the Giant Monster Ye'iitsoh, chips of his flint armor go flying. Seeing this, the Elder Twin says, "Let us gather those flint flakes. Our people can use them." Agreeing, the other Twin says: "That way we can turn Ye'iitsoh's evil into something good" (DB, p. 220). Similar use was made of the Bird Monsters, whose children were made into eagles and owls as they now exist, and later (in an adventure with Bat Woman) their feathers became all the different small birds as we know them (DB, pp. 235–36).

I see strong moral implications here. First, *we are related to the evils we must destroy: they come from our own behavior.* Second, *these evils can be turned to good things.* It is worth noting here that not all the good things would seem particularly good to people outside the Navajo ways. The children of the Cliff Monster, for instance, become the carrion-eating Vultures, while the children of the Monsters Who Kill With Their Eyes become the Whippoorwills, to whom the Monster-Slayer says, "It will be your destiny to make things sound beautiful. It will be your fate to make the world a happy place when darkness falls, [reassuring] all who hear you that the Sun will rise in the morning and bring forth a new day" (DB, p. 247). The Navajo are no Pollyannas, but they seem to have relied less on negative commandments or fear of punishment than on the belief in achieving harmony by positive actions. Their stories touch directly on the fight which we as post-Columbians are now waging to tame certain monsters who are ambushing us in "our" world: Strip-Mining Monsters, Nuclear Waste Monsters, Urban Sprawl and Social Alienation, and Racial Fear Monsters.

In short, the Vulcan in Milton's myth of how things got into such bad shape, and the Monsters of the Navajo version, are always out there to be dealt with by those of us into whose world they have fallen, setting the fires that now blaze on all the continents of this earth, and sowing the ashes that will choke us if we do not turn them into something good. The stories of post-Columbians and of pre-Columbians are all vital to our understanding of where we are in 1992, five hundred years after Columbus dropped from the zenith like a falling star on that Caribbean isle, whose Indian name we will never know, and "enlightened" two continents in his shining path.

Herbs of Healing

American Values

in American Indian Literature

Minority/Majority Considerations

The history of empires is a funny thing, whether we are talking of literary or political empires. Six thousand years ago, two small "tribes" dwelt at the far margins of great empires, and unknown elders within those tribes fashioned stories made to create and preserve those tribes as communal wholes, to keep them in a good relation to the transhuman powers of the universe, and to give them strength to handle the great forces of empire that would destroy the special separate cultures of those tribes. Versions of the stories which they fashioned have survived the fall of the great empires—and those tribes, having canonized their stories and stayed themselves by keeping them alive, now dominate Planet Earth economically and culturally. One of those tribes, of course, was "Indo-European," the other was "Hebrew." Much revised, reinterpreted, added onto in astonishing ways, the Hebrew stories are now the "Judeo-Christian Bible," while the Indo-European ones include those of Homer, Shakespeare, Karl Marx, Charles Darwin, and Mark Twain. I wonder which of the marginal tribes of this last decade of the Twentieth Century of the Christian Messiah may now be composing the poetry which, six thousand years from now, will energize our galaxy—and I wonder whether those tribes now dwell on Planet Earth.

Culture-Wars

There are some Big Guns of American culture and politics who aim to shoot down "Minority Literature," claiming that it is trash unworthy of our classrooms, that conversing with it corrupts and keeps students from the uplifting morality of the "classical" books they ought to be spending time with.[1] Well (Gentle Readers), I want to introduce you to a few members of this family of monsters, so you can judge whether they are fit company for the next generation of Americans, to whom we stand *in loco parentis.* I will do this by setting certain "classic" poems beside others by contemporary American Indian writers, hoping this critical look will prove that the true values of America are just as vividly and richly present in the "ethnic" as in the classic poems. I think the comparison will show why American culture is enriched, not weakened, by opening the curriculum to these "new" regions of our heartland—regions which the Big Guns want us to think are deserts, but which I see as *lands of plenty, filled with herbs of healing.* To show this, I hope, may help end the war fomented by those old Gunslingers between "Minority Literature" and "Great Books." They want, being Gunslingers, to divide and conquer—but (I would ask) why shouldn't we unite, and live in freedom and plenty? Think what Columbus found, five hundred years ago, upon which we now feast, or with which we doctor ourselves: corn, potatoes, chocolate, pumpkins, potatoes, quinine, curare, *as well as* European wheat and whiskey; coyotes, raccoons, bison *as well as* imported Black Angus, Norway rats, and Arab steeds; bluejays and scissortails *as well as* English sparrows, starlings, and pigeons for the shoulders of our bronzed panjandrums. Don't we want an *All-American* curriculum?

Family Values

To begin, we will set a much-anthologized poem, a "modern classic" by Wallace Stevens (1879–1955), alongside one by Simon Ortiz
(1941–) of Acoma Pueblo. These are small poems but they hold huge
ideas: versions of America itself. Stevens's "Anecdote of the Jar," first
published in 1923, has been given much commentary.[2] No such attention has yet been given "Speaking," published in the 1970s.[3]

Anecdote of the Jar	Speaking

I placed a jar in Tennessee,
And round it was, upon a hill,
It made the slovenly wilderness
Surround that hill.

The wilderness rose up to it,
And sprawled around no longer wild.
The jar was round upon the ground,
And tall and of a port in air.

It took dominion everywhere.
The jar was gray and bare.
It did not give of bird or bush,
Like nothing else in Tennessee.

I take him outside
under the trees,
have him stand on the ground.
We listen to the crickets,
cicadas, million years old sound.
Ants come by us.
I tell them,
"This is he, my son.
This boy is looking at you.
I am speaking for him."

The crickets, cicadas,
the ants, the millions of years
are watching us.
My son murmurs infant words,
speaking, small laughter
bubbles from him.
Tree leaves tremble.
They listen to this boy
speaking for me.

Stevens's poem is a terse fable, a kind of bonsai version of how
Art conquers and indeed enslaves Nature, or Reality. It is hard to
say whether Stevens approves, disapproves, or takes an ironically
detached view of this conquest. The poem certainly speaks in a Conqueror's voice, saying just what many American historians have said
(with no irony intended) about "civilizing" the "American Wilder-

ness," and compelling deference from its natives. Round, tall, and
with an important air, this non-natural Jar defines Wilderness as
slovenly, effortlessly tames it so that it "sprawl[s] around, no longer
wild," as the jar assumes imperial power "everywhere." Only in the
last three lines does Stevens seem to turn his irony against the Jar,
describing it as "gray and bare," as not allowing any sense of Nature
or Vegetation, and showing up the whole of "Tennessee" as being
UNlike the Jar—which indeed is "like nothing else in Tennessee."

There is, then, an Idea of Art and America in this poem—and
the idea, I think, is as purple, showy and poisonous as loco-weed.
Perhaps Stevens is himself appalled or ironically critical of this Empire of Abstract Ideas and the Jar which is their Centurion—yet the
poem exalts the magic of Abstraction and Power which enslaves
Tennessee and its creatures. One of the poem's crimes, indeed, is
its dandiacal condescending to the great abstract "state" of Tennessee—which, before that Jar arrived, was some sort of Tabula Rasa,
but after its arrival is cowed into cooliedom, kowtowing to the Imperial—nay, the DIVINE!—Artist. Just one bit of European Craft,
wrought by a single sly-and-handy poet, has turned an entire country into a subdued and self-alienated place, where his Viceroy refuses all resemblance to any "native" being!

It is of course a "classic" European notion that setting a Jar—or
a Cross, or a Crown, or a Writ—upon a hill allows one to "take
possession" of the whole "territory" surrounding that artifact. What
bothers me most, I think, is that Stevens does not really put any
America around his Jar. It was Gertrude Stein who wittily complained about Oakland, "There is no THERE, there!" In Stevens's
poem, there is no Tennessee in Tennessee: what's "there" is an East-
erner's idea that "culture stops at the Hudson" (a phrase actually
spoken to me once, with amused seriousness, by a professor of German at Amherst College).[4] Here the European Modern has throned
itself at the continent's center, destroying any possible alternative:
has, in short, "civilized" America.

But there IS an alternative, and Simon Ortiz has given us an
Acoma story that counters this "classic" one. His poem, "Speaking," like Stevens's "Anecdote," is short and profound. Its ideas of

America, of Art, of Nature and Humanity, are no less heroic in size, but lack the pompous arrogance, the neurofibromatosis of the artistic ego, which mask the Stevens poem.

One crucial difference is that Ortiz puts two humans into his poem, a father and his son. The poet himself is just as powerfully "there" as in Stevens—but whereas Stevens makes the Jar his Viceroy, Ortiz acts as Intercessor for his son, speaking "for" the infant to the powerful, ancient, and enduring beings whom this poem calls to our awareness. Then Ortiz is in turn "spoken for" by his infant son, whose language is after all older than that of his father, and whose "speaking" is listened to by those future generations to whom, eventually, he will indeed "speak for" his father.

And here we touch the nub of our comparison: it is FAMILY VALUES which dominate the Ortiz poem, *and the family in question is more than human.* "Anecdote of the Jar" narrates conquest, enslavement, culture-wars, class alienation, war between the Civil and the Natural, all as a result of the poet's imagined action. In "Speaking," the poet is not alone, not alienating himself by language or art, but using speech within a family, introducing his new son to other members of that family: trees, ground, crickets, cicadas, ants, and—in a startling leap—Time itself, the "millions of years." As the title tells us, this poem is about the human act of speaking, not just the high-culture *art* of speech or poetry, which is only one part of that more profound act. Here, the act of speaking and the art of listening work together in a mutual effort to gain understanding, support, and blessing for a fruitful life on earth. More remarkably, the poem discovers for its composer that his son's first speech to this great family is as deeply meaningful and important as anything his father can say. That a child's voice utters itself, that it is heard, is after all the most important human truth celebrated in the poem: to continue, to keep the human race alive, is more important than whatever the father might have uttered at that point. Implicitly, the poem humbles its poet AND us, tells us that our best speaking begins with, depends upon, is like that of the tiniest infant in this great universe.

So the idea of America in Ortiz's poem is truly a healing reminder of what is amiss in the remarkable poem by Stevens, where abstraction disdainfully dominates nature. The English of Ortiz is no less metaphysically sophisticated than that of Stevens, but it is "ordinary" English not "artful," it sounds like plain speech, not highfalutin rhetoric. As Wordsworth said in his Preface to the *Lyrical Ballads*, it is the language of real men speaking with deep feeling and not falling into "poetic diction." The result is a sense that Ortiz is just telling us a real story, what happened, what he did, what was said. In the poem, the poet stands not imperiously but humbly, not as lord of all he surveys but as an Acoma father, one member only of this realm of beings, conscious and respectful of those others we might scarcely notice "outside" our homes, including Time itself listening to the child as well as the father. This is no "taking possession" but a ritual of acknowledging smallness and dependency, fellowship and community, shared natural being. Stevens diagnoses an illness; Ortiz enacts a cure.

Speaking of Massacres

Human beings, however, do not always "share natural being" so nicely as the Ortiz poem shows them doing. John Milton (1608–1674), for instance, lived in interesting times, when one tribe of Europeans was apt to massacre another on religious grounds if no strictly economic or political excuse came handy. In 1655, certain Catholic troopers in the Savoy Alps slaughtered a large number of Protestant men, women, and babies, whereupon Milton—a Protestant—wrote a magnificent sonnet of protest, saying some pretty nasty things about the Pope and his forces.[5] Three and a half centuries afterwards, in 1890, a slaughter of similar brutality was carried out in Wounded Knee, South Dakota, by troopers of the U.S. Seventh Cavalry (George Custer's regiment)—their motive for massacre being also, in part, religious: the Lakotas slaughtered there were engaging in a forbidden religious ritual (the "Ghost Dance"), and the Lakota were not merely "heretics" but "heathens." In the 1970s (some fourscore and seven years later), the Hopi/Miwok poet Wendy Rose wrote a protest, Miltonic in its eloquence though not in its rhetoric, against the Wounded Knee Massacre. Let's see what we can learn from these two poems, starting with John Milton's sonnet.[6]

On the Late Massacre in Piedmont

Avenge, O Lord, thy slaughtered saints, whose bones
Lie scattered on the Alpine mountains cold—
Even them who kept thy truth so pure of old,
When all our fathers worshipped stocks and stones!
Forget not: in thy Book record their groans
Who were thy sheep, and in their ancient fold
Slain by the bloody Piedmontese, that rolled
Mother with infant down the rocks; their moans
The vales redoubled to the hills, and they
To heaven. Their martyred blood and ashes sow
O'er all the Italian fields, where still doth sway
The Triple Tyrant: that from these may grow
A hundred fold, who having learnt thy Way,
Early may fly the Babylonian woe!

When I talk with students about this poem, I speak of its biblical majesty of sound, of the history that lies behind and within it, its political commitment, the effective propaganda in its picture of mother and baby as they are brutally, callously, sadistically ROLLED down the steep Alpine slopes on those rocks. I marvel at how vividly we hear what happens in these mountain vales, the echoing moans of pain and screams of terror as women clinging to their babies are jerked, thrown, shoved over the precipices to fall down and down onto rocks below, how precisely Milton recreates in the poem's rhythm and cadences what the soldiers did. Then I try to say how much more powerful the poem becomes, how its words light up, when we connect them to their biblical reservoirs of prophetic rage, the thunderous lines of Isaiah, of the Psalms, of the book of Revelations. But I make sure we remember, in all this, where the poem "comes out" in the end: not in a call for God to slaughter the Catholics in return for their slaughter of Protestants, but in a call for God to RECORD the martyrdom and SPREAD THE NEWS of it, so that the blood of these martyrs will become the seed of a hundred times as many new believers converted by such unjustified suffering. These new Protestants will thereafter, having learned God's true Way, FLEE the coming destruction of the Roman church, which Milton refers to as a *Babylonian woe*—that is, the kind of woe suffered by the citizens of ancient Babylon when it fell, as described in Old and New Testaments. Milton expects his readers to know both the canonical books of the Bible, and the contemporary political uses of that canon. It is a very beautiful poem, majestic in its wrath, angelic in its compassion, apostolic in its looking toward an ultimate triumph of the despised and suffering minority to which its writer belongs.

For let me repeat: though the poem seems at first to call down the wrath of God upon the Roman Catholics, in the end it steadfastly awaits God's grace to draw these criminals into the faith of those they are murdering, and expresses hope that the converted people will then manage to flee the inevitable destruction which (Milton implies) will strike down this "Babylon"—this great imperial city of the Triple Tyrant. We have to see that Milton's great flashing thunderclouds call a gentle rain of mercy down from heaven, not just the thunder and lightning of prophetic wrath.

And now let us look at Wendy Rose's poem of protest:

I Expected My Blood and My Skin to Ripen

[When the blizzard subsided four days later, a burial party was sent to Wounded Knee. A long trench was dug. Many of the bodies were stripped . . . to get the ghost shirts . . . the frozen bodies were thrown into the trench stiff and naked. . . . only a handful of items remain in private hands . . . exposure to snow has stiffened the leggings and moccasins, and all the objects show the effects of age and long use. . . . " There follows: *Moccasins at $140, hide scraper at $350, buckskin shirt at $1200, woman's leggings at $275, bone breastplate at $1000.*—Plains Indian Art: Sales Catalog by Kenneth Canfield, 1977]

> I expected my blood and my skin
> to ripen,

not be ripped from my bones;
like green fruit I am peeled,
tasted, discarded; my seeds are stepped on
and crushed
as if there were no future. Now
there has been
no past. My own body gave up the beads,
my own arms handed the babies away
to be strung on bayonets, to be counted
one by one like rosary stones and then
to be tossed to each side of life
as if the pain of their borning
had never been.
My feet were frozen to the leather,
pried apart, left behind—bits of flesh
on the moccasins, bits of papery deerhide
on the bones. My back was stripped
of its cover, its quilling intact; was torn,
was taken away, was restored.
My leggings were taken like in a rape
and shriveled to the size of stick figures
like they had never felt
the push of my strong woman's body
walking in the hills.
It was my own baby whose cradleboard I held.
Would've put her in my mouth
like a snake
if I could, would've turned her
into a bush or old rock
if there'd been enough magic
to work such changes. Not enough magic
even to stop the bullets.
Not enough magic
to stop the scientists.
Not enough magic
to stop the collectors.

Rose's poem differs much from Milton's. His is spoken in the
poet's own voice; hers is a dramatic monologue spoken a long time

after the Wounded Knee massacre by one of the women killed there. Milton's poem says nothing of the economic forces involved in the Catholic/Protestant wars, though his *Lycidas* and prose tracts had shown his keen awareness of ecclesiastical corruptions in his time. But Wendy Rose prefaces her poem with a prose bit taken from a sales catalog written as guide to buyers and sellers of "Indian artifacts," some of which apparently were taken from corpses at Wounded Knee in 1890. The catalog offers quite a perspective on the teaching of American History in our schools. That the items described could be displayed, bought and sold on the open market, has its own grisly interest. To ask a controversial but (I think) relevant question, would it be possible to catalogue and sell a collection of souvenirs from Belsen, Dachau, or Auschwitz, and not draw a firestorm of outrage from a wide range of United States citizens? The answer to that question might explain why we may build in Washington, D.C., a monument to the Holocaust carried out in Europe by the Germans, but none to the many exterminations on this continent by the United States.

Though Rose's poem has for remote ancestor the biblical laments, it seems closer to the Martyr's Speech, particularly the Lament of Mary, Mother of Jesus. Perhaps the Middle English *Stond well, mother, under Rood* would have been the nearest "classic" poem for comparison—but it goes better with the historically parallel sonnet by Milton, which likewise concerns a particular slaughter for religious (and politico-economic) reasons of a minority group. One great difference between Rose and Milton is that she does not have his confidence that the martyrs' cause will prevail. Her speaker is defeated and lacks the tacit consolation apparent in Milton that from each of the martyred persons there will grow a multitude of "descendants" who will keep to the right way until the Apocalypse. She lacks, too, any sense that this painful death will allow her people to gain some sort of paradise, or regain America as the Ghost Dance had promised. Behind Rose's poem, no Scripture looms; it forms its own canon. Milton calls on God; Rose's unvoiced appeal is to her readers, to do the right thing to those who acted and still act against her people.

Rose expects her readers to know the history of Wounded Knee, and to have some remaining belief that what we call Art is linked in some way to the ethical and spiritual aspects of life, not solely to the monetary. As a medievalist, I know that cathedrals were built, in considerable part, by money drawn from saint-seeking tourists: religion, art, money are not separate from each other in Christian history. But it is less clear how the sufferings of women and children at Wounded Knee are related to the ART of that sales catalog, that "history" of the Collectors, the Museums, the Archaeologists and Scientists. And the only word Rose has for the Indian side of the encounter is MAGIC—not just that of the Ghost Dance, though including it. When I talk about this poem with students, one of the things I point to is the power of her final section's repeating the phrase, "not enough magic to stop . . . ," and how the "enemy list" builds to that final horror, from *bullets* to *scientists* to *collectors*. And with that last term, the poem has come full circle from its epigraph and made its point with the most poignant irony.

Men and Women: Garden and Wilderness

For our third pairing we have a complex sonnet by Robert Frost ("Never Again Would Birds' Song Be the Same") and a vivid, disturbing poem by Louise Erdrich ("Jacklight"). They are subtle in different ways about the relations between men and women: Frost puts a spin on the myth of Eden and our First Parents Adam and Eve, while Erdrich begins with the macho world of deerhunters (who use jacklights to mesmerize their prey) and turns it into the mythic world of Deer Woman (who lures men into a kind of Underworld). Here, first, is Frost's sonnet:

Never Again Would Birds' Song Be the Same

He would declare and could himself believe
That the birds there in all the garden round
From having heard the daylong voice of Eve
Had added to their own an oversound,

Her tone of meaning but without the words.
Admittedly an eloquence so soft
Could only have had an influence on birds
When call or laughter carried it aloft.
Be that as may be, she was in their song.
Moreover her voice upon their voices crossed
Had now persisted in the woods so long
That probably it never would be lost.
Never again would birds' song be the same.
And to do that to birds was why she came.

And here, next, is Erdrich's poem:

Jacklight

[The same Chippewa word is used both for flirting and hunting game, while another Chippewa word connotes both using force in intercourse and also killing a bear with one's bare hands.—R. W. Dunning, *Social and Economic Change among the Northern Chippewa* (1959)]

We have come to the edge of the woods,
out of brown grass where we slept, unseen,
out of knotted twigs, out of leaves creaked shut,
out of hiding.

At first the light wavered, glancing over us.
Then it clenched to a fist of light that pointed,
searched out, divided us.
Each took the beams like direct blows the heart answers.
Each of us moved forward alone.

We have come to the edge of the woods,
drawn out of ourselves by this night sun,
this battery of polarized acids,
that outshines the moon.

We smell them behind it
but they are faceless, invisible.
We smell the raw steel of their gun barrels,
mink oil on leather, their tongues of sour barley.
We smell their mothers buried chin-deep in wet dirt.

We smell their fathers with scoured knuckles,
teeth cracked from hot marrow.
We smell their sisters of crushed dogwood, bruised apples,
of fractured cups and concussions of burnt hooks.

We smell their breath steaming lightly behind the jacklight.
We smell the itch underneath the caked guts on their clothes.
We smell their minds like silver hammers
cocked back, held in readiness
for the first of us to step into the open.

We have come to the edge of the woods,
out of brown grass where we slept, unseen,
out of leaves creaked shut, out of our hiding.
We have come here too long.

It is their turn now
their turn to follow us. Listen,
they put down their equipment.
It is useless in the tall brush.
And now they take the first steps, not knowing
how deep the woods are and lightless.
How deep the woods are.

Frost's sonnet, as I read it, is a love poem, delicately praising the way
the natural unfallen voice of one human being has given the whole
world a hidden reservoir of partly human, partly animal music.[7] Erdrich's is a poem about sexual confrontation as well as the conflicts
in American culture between human and animal, technological and
natural—and it may hint at whites "preying on" American Indians
as well.

   In Frost's sonnet, someone (the poet? a son of Adam and Eve?) "reports" to us what Adam used to say about the way Eve's voice has
become "an oversound," which lives on in the song of birds now
that (the reporter implies) Eve herself is no longer with us. As Adam
asserts in the poem's last two lines, "Never again would birds' song
be the same. / And to do that to birds was why she came." Frost
has carefully distanced himself, not only from the Adam who thus
reminisces, but from whichever daughter or son of Adam reports

the reminiscing. More subtly, Frost has that reporter keep his or her own distance, remarking with wry amusement that HE (Adam, not the reporter) would declare such things. And even Adam seems to be mildly skeptical, since we are not told he *actually believed*, but only that he *could himself believe* what he is saying. So the reporter seems to be hinting wry disbelief or even cynical doubt of any truth in Adam's fancy: it was, well, the sort of thing Adam *would* say when he was going on about how wonderful things were in the *good* old days. In short, Frost's poem hedges Adam's fancy with so many thickets of skepticism, amused doubt, lightly patronizing headshakes, that the reader must suspect this Adam is pretty well past it, an old man telling tall tales that he has begun to take more seriously now that he is growing senilely sentimental.

Yet through all these ironic thorns, so carefully planted by Frost around his adamant fancy, there wafts a certain Edenic fragrance. The rhetorical hedges have been planted to guard a private space, not to institutionalize Adam as a loony old liar. Frost is a very subtle and tricky poet and easier to under-read than his sunlit words make it seem. His poem, however wondrous its spins and twists and leaps of poetic rhetoric, is charged with intense and yearning love for a woman who has changed the way the whole universe presents itself to him. This most shy and private man gets it both ways: any sensitive reader who has tried to celebrate his beloved without being a kiss-and-tell fool, or (worse) a sentimental pretender, will admire Frost's managing to tell the whole world what he feels with such humorous indirection that he could walk out of any courtroom unconvicted even though the jury would know the poem's "He" is really the poet's "I" in ambush. "He would declare," the poem begins: only after a rereading or two do we realize that this "He" is Adam speaking of Eve, and only after a few more readings do we understand that it is also Robert Frost speaking of his wife.[8] I know no more poignant love poem in English than this, and I would forgive any mistake in tone this poet might have made anywhere—and critics are fond of finding them, or inventing if necessary—for this wonderful sonnet. At any rate—so it seems to me—Frost gives us a beautiful and comforting reminder of what love in the Western tradition might once have been like.

Erdrich, in contrast, gives us a vivid and disturbing reminder of how unlike this ideal the relations between men and women too often are. Her poem's speakers seem to be the animals (for simplicity I will call them "deer") being hunted by humans with the help of a jacklight—illegal but effective, since the deer are hypnotized and come slowly and hesitantly out of the dark woods toward the hunters' guns. But when the deer get close enough to smell the hunters, what they learn is not just about these male hunters, but about their women, families, relationships. The deer smell guns, mink-oiled boots, beer-tainted breath; but they also smell the oppressed mothers of these men, their overworked and defeated fathers ("teeth cracked from hot marrow" suggests that the fathers too were hunters, but that the excesses have damaged them), their abused sisters. Something sinister (from the point of view of the hunters) is going on here: the deer are "walking in their souls," learning the nature of their lives beyond this hunting relationship. Even though the deer are sensing the cocked guns, it is to those cocked minds ("like silver hammers"), ready to send a bullet into the first deer to step into the open, that the deer are paying sharpest attention.

And now the poem, and this relationship, begin to turn around. When the speaker, for the third time, says, "*We have come to the edge of the woods,*" and describes once more, as if hypnotized, where they have come from, "out of our hiding," this time she follows with a very different assertion: "*We have come here too long.*" For anyone reading this poem aloud, here is the place to change the voice from tranced to grimly alert, here is where the speaker begins to take charge of the situation. "It is their turn now, / their turn to follow us," the woods-creature says—and if I were reading this aloud, I would want it to sound like the Godfather making an offer not to be refused: a quiet, deadly, utterly assured tone is what we should hear in these last sentences as the deer describe how the mesmeric hunters have themselves been hypnotized.

And at this point we may wonder just what these "woods" ARE, into which Erdrich's creatures are luring the hunters. Recalling Stevens's "slovenly wilderness," we may think these woods are that very wilderness, rising up like Tecumseh against its "possessors"; and there is partial truth to this. That is, Erdrich's hunters, though more

honkytonking Cowboys than hoity-toity Conquistadores, are "taking dominion" just as arrogantly as did Stevens's Jar. It is clear from
Erdrich's epigraph that a main theme of her poem will be ways in
which male contempt for women is shown in both language and
customs of hunting, whether practiced at deer-stand or bar-stool,
with jacklight or strobe lights. So luring deer to the jacklight becomes a figure for the luring of women to the sexual encounter, in
both cases to "score," or as one might say in Chippewa (according
to Dunning as cited by Erdrich in the epigraph to "Jacklight") to
"use force in intercourse" or to "kill a bear with one's bare hands"—
we need not try to cite the English slang equivalents of these Chippewa terms, but if we recall macho terms for dealing sexually with
women we know there are such equivalents.

I have not paired Frost and Erdrich to put down one or the other,
but I do think that alongside Erdrich's Honkytonk Horror-Babes we
may see Frost's Edenic portrait of Woman—her voice so "soft" that
only when she is calling out or laughing does it reach the birds
in the treetops—as offering a few too many sweets to the sweet.
But it is perhaps also true that Erdrich's Life-on-the-Rez portrait of
Macho Man Unmanned is less a poem of healing than a celebration
of power, and power used to capture and control—a reversal rather
than finding a good way. Still, I like the way each poem does its
thing, and the thing each poem does.

Old English, New English: Unriddling America

I want now to do something immodest: to show that it is possible
for a contemporary poet—in this case, myself—to use the "classical"
forms of English poetry to "say things" about this world, now, and
yet (I hope) be readable. It happens that my Irish and Scotch-Irish
mother's father, shortly before he died, told me to go to college (he
himself had got only into the third grade when he had to drop out
and work on his father's farm in the Ozarks). I admired and loved my
grandfather greatly—he was always good to me, good to work alongside, good to go on walks with, a man who never lied, and though
he could act a fool when he drank too much, a man whose judgment

was trusted by everybody most of the time and whose heart was trusted at all times. So when Aleck Camp told me to go to college, they would have had to kill me to prevent it; and of course nobody tried to stop me, everybody did what was possible to help me. But we had no money, nobody in the family had been to college, and getting there was no sure or easy thing.

Still, I made it. That is, a lot of people lifted me up to that dazzling window and cheered me for climbing through it. And once I got to college and jumped through the necessary hoops to clothe myself in a sheepskin, the great teachers at the University of Tulsa put me up for a Rhodes Scholarship and that was given me and so I got over to Oxford University, and to get the B.A. in English Literature there I had to study Old English language and literature, had to learn how the Old English alliterative meter works, had to memorize accidence and morphology and phonology and all that, so we could read *Beowulf* and *Dream of the Rood* and other poems. Later, in Yale Graduate School, I wrote a dissertation on Middle English alliterative poetry, and since then have taught History of the English Language and medieval literature a lot.

And one semester—you probably wondered where all this was going, and here I hope you will see it is getting to the point—I had to fill in for a younger teacher, Tom Goodman, who is much better at Old English than I am, when he was called out of town that day, and the class that day happened to be considering some of the Old English poems called Riddles. With these I had a nodding acquaintance, had worked through some of the less tough ones. But now suddenly I had to face a group of students and not disgrace myself while talking with them about the "Book" and "Swan," and others of the Riddles in which whatever creature the poet taps must tell the listener/reader in enigmatic ways its life story. Here, for instance, is the magnificent "Swan," who speaks to us from the *Exeter Book* (written around A.D. 950–1000), as I translate its chant:

The Swan's Song

Garbed in silence	I go on earth,
dwell among men	or move on the waters.
Yet far over halls	of heroes in time

> my robes and the high   air may raise
> and bear me up   in heaven's power
> over all nations.   My ornaments then
> are singing glories   and I go in song
> bright as a star   unstaying above
> the world's wide waters,   a wayfaring soul.

It would be a grave mistake to think one had "solved" the riddle of this poem by saying, "Swan!" The Old English poet surely meant us not just to listen to each clue as the poem unfolds, and gradually deduce who is speaking to us here. We certainly are meant to go through that process, to observe that this creature telling its life story lives in silence among human beings or on the water; but then it takes to the air, rises far above human habitations and looks down from that height on those, even the most heroic of them, dwelling below; and when it moves at that height its ornaments (which the Old English original implies are the same as its "robes") "sing" and "shine," so that in flight it moves in glory that is beyond the mortal heroes on earth. And we are surely meant to see with astonishment in the poem's last few words that this earth-mute, heaven-musical traveler is a pilgrim soul. That is, everything in the poem comes together in those last few words, and we see this "swan" is an emblem of the immortal soul which in its flesh is relatively mute and slow and likely to be held of little account, but when it rises to its heavenly destination makes part of the angelic choir, going in glorious music toward the throne of God, its wayfaring at last reaching that place of power and beauty far beyond the palaces and thrones of human monarchs and heroes.

In translating, I have pretty much kept Old English alliterative meter: each line has two half-lines, each half-line has two strong stresses. So every line will have at least four stresses, and at least two of these must alliterate. It is the number three stress—that is, the first stress of the second half-line—which is the key to any line: stress 3 *must* alliterate with either 1 or 2, or with both of them. In "The Swan," for instance, line 1 alliterates on the /g/ of stresses 1 and 3: *GARBED in Silence   I GO on earth*. In line 8, the alliterative stresses are 2 and 3 (*bright as a STAR   unSTAYing above*), although there is extra alliteration also between stresses 1 and 4 (*BRIGHT, aBOVE*), an effect I like more than did Old English poets, probably.

But now comes the immodest part: I want to show that this old Anglo-Saxon poetic form is still alive, will still blossom and fruit if planted deep and watered from Indian springs. What has to be done is the same as with any ancient form: treat it with respect, not as entertainment but as revelation. I have said elsewhere that the Old English poems usually called "riddles" are meant to call before the reader certain astonishing created beings in this universe and let them speak their spiritual dimensions, cleanse the doors of perception and bare the witty ligatures by which things are put together, held together, pass into and out of human comprehension.[9] The Old English poet gives them their voices and lets them re-member themselves for us, coax us into re-cognizing them. If we want to write a "New English" Riddle, we need to try and give the creatures of our time such voices and dimensions, we have to realize that in our everyday life there are amazing and mysterious convergings of power and mystery: as Wordsworth said in his great Immortality Ode, we are "moving about in worlds not realized." If a house spoke its being, it would tell of its power to summon the dead Beethoven's majestic music, or the ghosts of dead movie stars to dance or machine-gun or sing us to sleep; any house could tell us how within it the great rivers rise to our lips in drinkable water, spray over our heads in cleansing coolness, flush away the grime and filth of our daily lives. Or we could ask a Television Set—say a Sony from Japan—to speak its mundane mysteries to us:

On this azure eyeball   where hell twice raised
its monstrous mushrooms,   my mind's eye opened
as the holster hardened   for its hot ghost-gun
from barrels of black   dinosaur-blood; shortly,
on floating steel,   men steered me eastward
through a gate of gold,   gave me then
to an iron horse   that hauled me here,

```
unpacked me and pinned        upon my backside
a long tail, tipped          with metallic teeth.
A woman acquired me,          carried me home,
set me high on an altar       for adoration,
drove Dracula teeth           into tight joyholes,
touched me until              she turned me on—
I reached into heaven         and handed her down
from its ether Caruso's       heart in a clown-suit,
spread time at her toes       like a tiger's skin
until she yawned,             touched me again,
and I went blind.             I bless FAR-SEERS
who know my name              and now will speak it!
```

I have followed the Old English poets in using enigmatic metaphors ("kennings") like *azure eyeball* for Planet Earth, and *monstrous mushrooms* for the bomb-clouds over Hiroshima and Nagasaki. I "transfigured" the TV's cathode-ray tube as a "hot ghost-gun" —it "shoots" arrays of electrons at a "target" screen and evokes "ghosts"; in fact, since actors and historical figures on our TV screens often are long dead, their TV icons are ghosts as nearly "real" as we can live with. And since the TV case or frame is made of plastic from polymerized petroleum, I figure it as "holster" for a "ghost-gun," and call the oil "dinosaur-blood"—not much of a far-fetch, considering the old green dinosaur on the Sinclair signs: advertising people are more poetic than plenty of our poets.

The poem won't "work" unless readers have fun figuring it out— not only as a kind of game but as a way of getting into what marvelous magical things a TV set really is and does. Poems, like jokes, work best if they don't need explaining, but unlike jokes they can be effective more than once (though differently)—and even, I would claim, *after* being explained.[10] The old *Reader's Digest* pieces are not so far from the Old English Riddles: "I am Joe's Kidney," for instance. And the poem ought to do something else besides give a Nintendo-like play-pleasure; it ought to be informative, the reader ought to come away saying: Well, that's true, I see some things now better than before, and maybe some things I didn't see before—things look a little different, a little clearer and interlocking now. Teach and delight, as Horace said: that's what I sort of hoped would happen once

the reader got through the more simple "floating steel" (the paradox
of those huge steel ships, which we forget "ought" never to float)
and Golden Gate and Iron Horse, and fetched up on that tail and
its teeth. I hoped the teasing and fun of what the woman was doing
was like what some of the Old English poets did with their double
entendres, and I hoped those Dracula teeth in "joyholes" would be
clear enough metaphors for the plug and socket. After all, we get
a lot of joy—or we expect to—from those electric outlets in our
living rooms.

Then I "reversed" the usual direction of the metaphoric shift when
the TV says the woman "touched me until she turned me on"—to
"turn on" somebody was a cliché of Beats and Hippies, so I had fun
letting a TV speak it literally of itself. And once "turned on" a TV
does literally "reach into heaven" to collect its images, it "hands
down" from the "ether" an old recording of, say, Caruso singing in *I
Pagliacci*, so that a TV set "kills" time, makes a "trophy" of it like
a tiger-skin. I thought that notion might justify the TV's saying it
"spread time like a tiger's skin" at the feet of the woman viewing
such old scenes. (Yes, the old rhyme about Elinor Glyn was running
through my head at that point: "Would you rather sin / With Elinor
Glyn / On a tiger skin . . . ?") And last, I had fun translating the
Greek/Latin TELE-("far") VISION ("seeing") into FAR-SEERS, telly-
viewers. The in-joke here is that an Old English poet might "give
away" the solution to one of these "riddles" by writing its name in
ancient runes instead of the Latin-derived alphabet used for most of
the poem. So FAR-SEER in capital letters is a clue to this riddle's
"solution"—*TV SET*.

But Old English poetic form will hold less technology-driven
points. So let me end this essay with one short and one slightly
longer example of how I have tried to use the alliterative Riddle
genre, adapting WAS poetics for American Indian themes and purposes.[11] Here is the short piece, which I hope needs no commentary:

Birch Canoe

Red men embraced	my body's whiteness,
cutting into me	carved it free,
sewed it tight	with sinews taken

from lightfoot deer   who leaped this stream—
now in my ghost-skin   they glide over clouds
at home in the fish's   fallen heaven.

And finally, I have tried to compose one Riddle in gratitude for the gift of eagle feathers, given me by Bob and Evelyne Voelker when I was elected to the Board of Directors of the American Indian Center of Mid-America. I asked a friend, Dale Besse, to bead these into an Eagle Fan, which I carry when I dance; since the late 1970s I have been a Gourd Dancer. The poem tells how an eagle in flight pierces clouds just as a beadworker's needle goes through beads and the white buckskin of the fan's handle, spiralling round sky and fan; and how the eagle flies from dawn to sunset, linking colors of day and night as they are linked on a Gourd Dancer's blanket (half crimson, half blue), and just as they are beaded onto the handle of the Eagle Fan. In the poem, ordinary things are given mysterious names: tree leaves are green light-dancers, wood is tree-heart or ash-heart, clouds are thrones of thunder-beings. Readers may like to name for themselves what I have called a "one-eyed serpent with silver-straight head."

What the Eagle Fan Says
(For the Voelkers, the Besses, and all the Dancers.)

I strung dazzling thrones   of thunder beings
on a spiraling thread   of spinning flight,
beading dawn's blood   and blue of noon
to the gold and dark   of day's leaving,
circling with Sun   the soaring heaven
over turquoise eyes   of Earth below,
her silver veins,   her sable fur,
heard human relatives   hunting below
calling me down,   crying their need
that I bring them closer   to Wakonda's ways,
and I turned from heaven   to help them then.
When the bullet came,   it caught my heart,
the hunter's hands   gave earth its blood,

loosened light beings and let us float
toward the sacred center of song in the drum,
but fixed us first firm in song-home
that green light-dancers gave to men's knives,
ash-heart in hiding where deer-heart had beat,
and a one-eyed serpent with silver-straight head
strung tiny rattles around white softness
in beaded harmonies of blue and red—
lightly I move now in a man's left hand,
above dancing feet follow the sun
around old songs soaring toward heaven
on human breath, and I help them rise.

Herbs of Healing

Not all healing herbs are sweet, and I have had some bitter observations to make in the discussions above. But I hope that it will be with us as with Peter Rabbit and his siblings: the camomile tea on the one hand, and the fresh blackberries and bread and milk on the other, are surely the right medicine in each case. I hope readers will have found the sweet and nourishing, the bitter and healing, in some measure in this essay. We are talking about a so far undiscovered country, five hundred years after Columbus mistook it for Japan or China or India or the Earthly Paradise. We are talking about some undiscovered writers whose work is good for this America. I wish you joy of it.

Notes

Walking among the Stars

Reprinted from *I Tell You Now: Autobiographical Essays by Native American Writers*, edited by Brian Swann and Arnold Krupat, by permission of the University of Nebraska Press. Copyright © 1987 by the University of Nebraska Press.

Buck Creek Community

1. For Tzi-To-Pah and Nom-peh-wah-the, see John Joseph Mathews, *The Osages: Children of the Middle Waters* (Norman: University of Oklahoma Press, 1961). The two were elders and leaders of the Little Osages from the mid nineteenth century; Nom-peh-wah-the's father, who had the same name, had led an Osage delegation to St. Louis about 1820 to request that a Jesuit priest be sent to their village; he had also perhaps been in an Osage delegation to Washington just after the Louisiana Purchase in 1803–4. Nom-pehwahthe's grandson, known as Chief Fred Lookout, was head chief of the Osages in the first half of the twentieth century. The name *Nompehwahthe* was given to me in 1952 by my grandmother Josephine Jump, who was of the Strikeaxe family and the Thunder clan, in a ceremony attended by Chief Lookout's descendants, who signed the presentation copy of John Joseph Mathews's *Talking To The Moon* given to me then.

Making a Name

1. The examples of Latin and common names cited in this essay come from Edward Howe Forbush, *A Natural History of American Birds*, rev.

John R. May (New York: Bramhall House, 1955). (Some of these species names have been replaced by newer ones.)

2. Forbush, *American Birds*, p. 41.

3. Forbush, *American Birds*, p. 282.

4. I hope the theory that birds developed from a particular group of dinosaurs stays credible, because I like to think of a robin as a tiny Tyrannosaurus who put on feathers and survived, who learned to sing and has human approval therefore, and who understands that when the stars dim and the sun brightens for us we move from the great mystery of infinity to the great mystery of here and now in a way only song can celebrate.

5. On the other hand, "slang" allows speakers to invent and re-invent any given name. It seems to show just how determined the natural human speaker is to keep language alive, to reinvent the wheel any time a hill is ready to be rolled down. We may have to say *telephone* in the boardroom, but in the coffeeshop we call it a *horn*, a *blower*, or more and better/worse things. And it is fascinating that computer language often begins as slang, or skis down into it: we do not speak of diodes or transistors but of "chips"— and we even produce Greco-English halfbreeds like "gigaflops" and "teraflops." The poetry of things, which engineers compose, is turning into the poetry of everyday language, because they have to use language for quick and dirty communication.

6. Likewise, a *Presbyterian* is simply an "elder"—our term *priest* being only a shortened form of *presbyter:* the Greek original as used in the New Testament meant one of the elders, more experienced older Christians whose age lent wisdom, since an older person had been born nearer to the time of Christ's still-recent life and death. The Presbyterian Church grew out of efforts to restore "primitive" (of the "first" or "prime" age) Christian church customs, purged of later Roman Catholic "innovations." Thus they rejected the church-rank of *bishop*, a term deriving from Greek *episkopos*, since they regarded that New Testament Greek word as simply referring to "overseers" or "supervisors"—because in Greek *episkopos* means just that, *epi-* "over" and *skop-* "see, look."

7. See Ralph K. Andrist, *The Long Death: The Last Days of the Plains Indian* (New York: Collier Books, 1964), section 2, "Massacre in Minnesota" (pp. 27–68), for an account of the 1862 Santee uprising and its effects.

8. Charles Alexander Eastman, *Indian Boyhood* (New York: Dover, 1972), pp. 51–52. (I consider this passage at greater length in the next chapter.)

9. Francis La Flesche, *A Dictionary of the Osage Language*, Smithsonian Institution, Bureau of American Ethnology Bulletin 109 (Washington, D.C., 1932).

10. I have discussed Osage ways in "Traditional Osage Naming Ceremonies: Entering the Circle of Being," in Arnold Krupat and Brian Swann, eds., *Recovering the Word: Essays on Native American Literature* (Berkeley: University of California Press, 1987), pp. 446–66.

11. "La Noche Triste," printed in April 1890 in Frost's high school literary magazine, and many later Frost poems dealing with Indians, are discussed by Frost's granddaughter, Dr. Lesley Lee Francis, in "Robert Frost and the Majesty of Stones Upon Stones," *Journal of Modern Literature* 9, 1 (1981/82): 3–26. In "Robert Frost and Susan Hayes Ward" (*Massachusetts Review* [Summer/Autumn 1985]: 341–50), she tells Frost's responses to the history of his ancestor Major Charles Frost (ca. 1631–97), who in 1676 by treachery sold into Caribbean slavery many Indians, and in 1697 was ambushed and killed by their survivors. After his burial, the Indians dug up his body, hung it from a stake, and danced around it till troops drove them off. The body was then reburied under an enormous boulder, and the Indians let it be.

12. Wilbur R. Jacobs, "British Indian Policies to 1783," in Wilcomb E. Washburn, ed., *History of Indian-White Relations*, Handbook of North American Indians, vol. 4 (Washington D.C.: Smithsonian Institution, 1988), p. 10: "During the bitter fighting in 1763–64 Gen. Jeffrey Amherst actually ordered that the Indians around Fort Pitt be infected with gifts of smallpox [laden] blankets. The Indian uprising failed, and Fort Pitt was easily relieved after a smallpox epidemic broke out among the warriors besieging the fort"; quoted in M. Annette Jaimes, ed., *The State of Native America* (Boston: South End Press, 1992), p. 12 n. 21. Told that a subordinate was obeying Amherst's orders to send smallpox-filled blankets among the Indians, Amherst wrote: "You will do well to [infect] the Indians by means of blankets as well as to try every other method that can serve to extirpate this execrable race." (L. Stiffarm and P. Lane, Jr., "The Demography of Native North America" in Jaimes, *State of Native America*, p. 32, citing [p. 50 n. 51] E. W. and A. E. Stearn, *The Effect of Smallpox on the Destiny of the Amerindian* [Boston: B. Humphries, 1945], pp. 44–45.) See also Helen Jaskoski, "'A Terrible Sickness Among Them': Smallpox and Stories of the Frontier," in *Early Native American Writing: New Critical Essays* (Cambridge: Cambridge University Press, 1996), pp. 136–57.

13. Stiffarm and Lane, "Demography," p. 32 n. 55, p. 50, say that blankets for Mandans were "sent upriver on the steamer *St. Peter's* [and] distributed by army personnel on June 19, 1837," citing Francis A. Chardon, *Journal at Fort Clark, 1834–39* (Pierre, South Dakota: State Historical Society of South Dakota, 1932).

14. The Osage areas of occupation and hegemony are described by Willard

H. Rollings in *The Osage, an Ethnohistorical Study of Hegemony on the Prairie-Plains* (Columbia: University of Missouri Press, 1992), especially chapter 5, "Osage Hegemony," and pp. 213–16. Mathews, *The Osages*, contains a map of areas controlled to 1808 by Osages on p. 88.

15. For the setting of "tribes" against each other in Missouri after 1804, used by the U.S. to force the treaty by which the Osages "ceded" most of their Missouri lands, see Rollings, *Osage*, pp. 220 ff.—especially pp. 230–31, mentioning attacks by the Sac, Mesquakie, Iowa and others which led to abandonment by the Osages of their Missouri village into which the 1808 treaty had "relocated" them, and pp. 235–36 detailing some of the invasions of Osage lands after the War of 1812 by Shawnee, Cherokee, Delaware, Piankashaw, and Peoria Indians who had been moved west by the U.S. in those years.

16. *The Aeneid*, book 8, lines 138ff; Virgil, *The Aeneid*, trans. Robert Fitzgerald (New York: Random House, 1983), p. 233.

History, Myth, and Identity among Osages and Other Peoples

1. Erik Erikson has argued for the importance of much later periods in an individual's life as crucial to shaping and reshaping identity; the long obituary notice in the *New York Times* (Friday, May 13, 1994) gives a very useful and interesting account of his work. It mentions, for instance, that his *Childhood and Society* (1950) was published after he had studied early childhood training of Sioux people and differentiated their children's identity-sense from that of the Yurok Indians whom he also studied. He proposed that humans undergo successive "identity crises" during their lives, and applied this notion to "psychobiographic" studies of Martin Luther and Mahatma Gandhi (1958, 1969). Erikson's having himself been an "in-betweener"—illegitimate child suspended between religions (Lutheran, Jewish), taunted by Nazis as a Jew, rejected at the synagogue as of Nordic appearance—and his studies of non-European identity-formation surely made him sensitive to issues with which one is faced in looking at the "autobiographies" of American Indians with which the present essay is concerned.

2. *Geronimo: His Own Story*, ed. S. M. Barrett, newly ed. by Frederick W. Turner, III (New York: E. P. Dutton, 1970). All kinds of problems are presented to us by this work: to what extent is it an accurate transcription or paraphrase of Geronimo's account, how far does its organization and sequencing reflect Barrett's rearranging of bits and pieces, how much was added or subtracted or altered by the intermediary Apache translators used by Barrett. I cut this Gordian knot by assuming the book as printed is au-

thentic and accurate enough for the purposes of this discussion, expressing reservations only here and there.

3. The 1993 movie called *Geronimo*, for instance, though "sympathizing" with Geronimo, presents him primarily as a larger-than-life Indian warrior fighting American soldiers; and the soldiers are presented as, of course, highly respectful of his courage, of the relatively just causes for which he was fighting, and so on. In the end, that movie asks us to understand Geronimo as "Apache" in only two dimensions: the fierce indomitable warrior, and the man unjustly treated by mean and crooked Mexicans and Americans. There is nothing whatever of Apache cosmology, theology, ideology, customs or ways except in relation to the "war with whites," which is pictured as about a homeland but not about a way of life or world-views.

4. *Geronimo*, p. 61. Barrett's version of Apache "creation time" is probably much distorted, but my point is that Geronimo began by telling some version of the Apache Creation Story as his introduction to the story of Geronimo. One may argue that the Christian Gospel of John distorts the Judaic account of the beginning of things, since it is a late Hellenized version adapted to provide a biography of a man taken by its author to be the Messiah. The Hellenizer, nevertheless, has reasons for providing that reference to the *Genesis* story.

5 "Dragon" of course carries all kinds of European baggage, but so does "Monster," a term more usual for translators of Apache, Navajo, or Pueblo Creation Stories, in which such episodes of "Monster-slaying" set parameters for the world as humans now know it. See, for instance, Paul Zolbrod's edition of the Navajo Creation Story, *Diné Bahanè* (Albuquerque: University of New Mexico Press, 1984).

6. *Geronimo*, p. 69. I wonder about the "literal meaning" that in Barrett's account is assigned to *Apache*, and suspect some confusion on Barrett's part.

7. *Geronimo*, p. 70. Could *No-doyohn* be a mistake for *Mogollon?*

8. See the earlier essay in this collection, "Making a Name," for qualifications of this.

9. Though the history of these words sheds light on the attitudes of Europeans toward "Indians" whom they civilized with such genocidal efficiency, there is not space to summarize that history here. A sketch is given in my "Why Shakespeare, Though Not Unselfish, Never Had Any Fun," in E. Cooley, Mervin R. Barnes, and John A. Dunn, eds., Papers of the Mid-America Linguistics Conference for 1978 (Norman: University of Oklahoma Press, 1979), pp. 478-487.

10. See the entry for *civilise* in the *Oxford English Dictionary*. The word

was Anglicized in the early 17th century precisely to justify man's ways to man as the British began to turn the globe a shocking Imperial pink: as Captain John Smith wrote of his experiences in Virginia, it was easier to civilize "them" by the sword than by fair means (to paraphrase the *OED* citation from his 1624 *History of Virginia*).

11. *Geronimo*, p. 49. One of the "fairs and expositions" was the St. Louis World's Fair of 1904, where he was exhibited as prisoner of war. He must have been in its headquarters, the newly built Brookings Hall of Washington University. I teach and have an office across the quadrangle from Brookings. Geronimo perhaps walked round the new-built quadrangle, where Commencement ceremonies now are held.

12. Jason Betzinez, *I Fought With Geronimo*, with W. S. Nye (Harrisburg, Penn.: The Stackpole Company, 1959). (Page references to this book are given parenthetically in the text.)

13. Morris E. Opler, *Apache Odyssey: A Journey between Two Worlds* (New York: Holt, Rinehart and Winston, 1969), p. x.

14. Eastman, *Indian Boyhood*, hereafter in this chapter cited by page number alone. As with Geronimo's autobiography, I leave aside the difficult question of how non-Indian input—in this case, from Eastman's white wife, herself a teacher whom he met while at Pine Ridge where she was teaching Sioux children—may have shaped and colored Eastman's account of his life as it stands in his printed work. I ignore also (for now) the neo-historicist aspects of the case: the shifting vogues and forms of Indian autobiography; the particular and general social tasks assigned by whites to this genre during the period 1890–1940 as part of dealing with post-Wounded Knee Indian tribal entities and the "Indian question" as a whole; and the ways Eastman himself fitted his autobiographical writing and speaking into such tasks and his own personal and ethnic agenda. The very useful discussions and bibliographic account of Indian autobiographies by scholars, especially Peter Beidler, Kathleen Sands, H. David Brumble and Arnold Krupat, are essential to the full discussion such questions deserve.

15. The account as here cited from *Indian Boyhood* misses the sacred dimension of such songs, which tie intricately into the Creation Stories— though certainly Eastman would have known that dimension well, so it is likely the inadequate understanding of Santee ways by his wife Elaine Goodale Eastman that caused this lacuna in Eastman's account. We can clearly see this sacred dimension in traditional Osage naming ceremonies, as printed in 1928 (with transcription, translation, introduction and detailed commentary) by Francis La Flesche in *The Osage Tribe: Two Versions of the*

Child-Naming Rite, Smithsonian Institution, Bureau of American Ethnology Annual Report, no. 43, 1924–1925 (Washington, D.C.: 1928), pp. 23–264. Other Osage ceremonies, which illustrate how members of this Siouan-language tribe were being educated at the time Eastman was growing up, are transcribed and translated by La Flesche as BAE Annual Reports numbers 36, pp. 35–597 (*Rites of the Chiefs, Sayings of the Ancient Men*); 39, pp. 31–630 (*Rite of Vigil*); 45, pp. 529–833 (*Rite of the Wa-xo-be*); and in the 1939 *BAE Bulletin* (*War Ceremony and Peace Ceremony of the Osage Indians*), *passim*. Some translations of songs and recital-chants from these ceremonies, and many useful glosses and definitions, are found in La Flesche's 1932 *Dictionary of the Osage Language*. And see, now, Garrick Bailey's account, *The Osage and the Invisible World* (Norman: University of Oklahoma Press, 1995).

16. La Flesche, *Osage Tribe*, pp. 56–58.

17. Ibid., p. 57. In Euroamerican culture, words like *electricity* and *gravity* have "literal," "figurative," and "scientific" sense-clusters. Alert and sensible readers negotiate among these flavors and quarky senses with no particular difficulty, and the same ability to negotiate among ceremonial and everyday, metaphysical and physical word-senses should be recognized among Osages and other Indian peoples. There are actual instances within some of the ceremonial recitations or narratives where the reciter will say things, in referring to the "journey from the stars to this earth," such as "They came to a valley: verily, it was not a valley"—warning the listeners, I believe, that the language being used is special, figurative, mysterious, not everyday.

18. I happened lately to look at the words *chameleon* and *chamomile* in the *American Heritage Dictionary* and was surprised to find the same Greek word is behind the first half of each. A *chameleon* is a "ground-lion," and the herb *chamomile* is a "ground-apple." The *AHD* editors say that behind the Greek *chameleon* is a Babylonian word which itself means "ground-lion," so the Greeks must have thought the Babylonians had a good name for that little reptile, and just translated the name into their own language. As for *chamomile*, it of course is not actually a ground-apple; rather, as the *AHD* editors say, some varieties *smell* like apples. I have my doubts about this, particularly since *melon* is the Greek word behind the *-mile* part of *chamomile*, and *melon* might refer to some fruit other than what we would call an "apple." Ah well—Sprachgeschmellers differ.

19. Of course, as discussed in "Making a Name," our English is far more transparent where machines and technology are concerned and our speakers are still coining names in spoken as well as literary English: we under-

stand *hatchback* or *Fuzzbuster* or *beeper* to be "tribal" words that are figurative, describing what they refer to.

20. Gene Weltfish, *The Lost Universe: Pawnee Life and Culture* (Lincoln: University of Nebraska Press, 1977); page references are cited in the text. A primary source, given by the Pawnee elder Tahirussawichi through the bilingual Pawnee scholar James Murie, transcribed and translated by Murie and Alice Fletcher, is printed as *The Hako: A Pawnee Ceremony*, Smithsonian Institution, Bureau of American Ethnology Annual Report, no. 22 (Washington, D.C., 1904). Fletcher for years had found no Omaha informants to recite for her the texts and songs of this intertribal ceremony, but at last located a Pawnee elder who knew and would recite it. I assume that since the Hako Ceremony was intertribal, each tribe performed it in its own language and particular format. The ceremony is an "adoption" rite in which two groups become "brothers." That it involves the sacred pipe suggests it may be one of the most important "peace" ceremonies of the pre-Columbian Great Plains tribes. Anglo accounts of Plains Indians seem always to stress their warfare, their hostilities and rivalries—making them sound very like the Europe known to history as a collection of rabidly hostile and murderous peoples always trying to slaughter or conquer or dominate each other. How the Indian nations succeeded in getting along, rather than how they conducted their warring or raiding relationships, is emphasized by Howard Meredith in *Dancing on Common Ground: Tribal Cultures and Alliances on the Southern Plains* (Lawrence: University of Kansas Press, 1995), discussing Southern Plains nations including Wichita, Pawnee, Caddo, Plains Apache, Cheyenne and Arapaho, and Comanche (see, for the annual Pawnee-Wichita Visitation, pp. 20–21, 58–59).

21. The Pawnee images of microcosm/macrocosm ought to be compared to those of the Europeans in about the same time-frame, say 1400–1600 A.D.—there are startling resemblances as well as the expected differences. Work by Chaucer, Spenser, and Shakespeare could be set beside Pawnee texts—though it would outrage Mono-culturists to anthologize *The Faerie Queene* along with *The Hako Ceremony*.

22. La Flesche, B.A.E. *Annual Report No. 36* (1921), p. 48.

23. See La Flesche, *Osage Tribe*, especially pp. 159, 162.

24. Ibid., p. 30.

25. Ibid., p. 31.

26. Ibid, pp. 56–57.

How Columbus Fell from the Sky and Lighted Up Two Continents

1. I wonder what might have been the social and political situation in North and Central America, had Europeans only been precisely five hundred years "behind schedule" in their social and technical development, so that Columbus might have landed on that Caribbean island on October 12, 1992. What might have been the populations, social structures, and technologies of the Central American nations—or indeed, of the native peoples of what is now the southeastern United States? When De Soto passed through in the 1500s, an extensive chiefdom called Coosa controlled a region more than two hundred miles long in the present states of Tennessee, Georgia, and Alabama; see Marvin T. Smith, "Indian Responses to European Contact: The Coosa Example," in *First Encounters: Spanish Explorations in the Caribbean and the United States, 1492-1570*, ed J. T. Milanich and S. Milbrath (Gainesville: University of Florida Press, 1989), pp. 135-49.

2. J. M. Cohen, ed. and trans., *The Four Voyages of Columbus* (Harmondsworth: Penguin, 1969), p. 118.

3. John Milton, *Paradise Lost*, ed. Scott Elledge (New York: Norton, 1975), book 1, lines 732-48.

4. Cohen, *Four Voyages*, p. 70.

5. Ibid., pp. 58, 60.

6. Ibid., p. 161.

7. Ibid., p. 121.

8. Ibid., p. 136-67.

9. Kirkpatrick Sale, *The Conquest of Paradise: Christopher Columbus and the Columbian Legacy* (New York: Plume, 1991), p. 134.

10. William Shakespeare, *King Henry V*, ed. T. W. Craik (London and New York: Routledge, 1995), act 3, scene 3, lines 5-43 (omitting lines 8-9, 15-18, 22-28, and 30-32). The description of Henry V as "the mirror of all Christian kings" is given by the Chorus before act 2 (line 6).

11. A "one-eyed Ford" is an old jalopy with one good headlight, celebrated in contemporary American Indian songs ("Forty-Nine Songs"). The Chippewa poet Diane Burns has a collection of poems called *Riding the One-Eyed Ford*.

12. The "first version" of Eve's creation by God is in Genesis 1:26-27, where God made both man and woman at the same time, in his own image, male and female. The "second version" is in Genesis 2:7-25, where God formed man out of the dust on the ground, put him (Adam) into the Garden

of Eden, and there anesthetized Adam and took a rib from his side, of which God fashioned Eve.

13. Michael E. Long, "Secrets of Animal Navigation," *National Geographic* 179, 6 (June 1991): 80, 95.

14. Ibid., p. 97.

15. Zolbrod, *Diné Bahanè*. Cited in this chapter as *DB*.

16. Of course the commentators on the biblical accounts have a great deal to say, but the Bible itself is very brief. Eve is said by Adam, after she has been fashioned from his rib, to be "bone of my bones, and flesh of my flesh: she shall be called Woman, because she was taken out of Man. Therefore shall a man leave his father and his mother, and shall cleave unto his wife: and they shall be one flesh" (Genesis 2:23–25). After the Fall, God tells Eve that (as punishment, it seems) he will "greatly multiply" her sorrow and her conception, adding: "Thy desire shall be to thy husband, and he shall rule over thee" (Genesis 2:16). These passages seem to say only that the husband/wife relation takes precedent over the husband/parents relation, and that wives must submit to being ruled by husbands.

Herbs of Healing

1. I am thinking of Allen Bloom, George Will, Dinesh D'Souza and their sort, whose approach to literary and cultural matters reminds me of words put by clever Oxonians into the mouth of the great Plato scholar Benjamin Jowett: *Here am I, my name is Jowett: / There is no knowledge but I know it. / I am the Master of this College—/ What I know not is not knowledge.* Or, again, they are like Jim arguing with Huck Finn about whether French is a human language or not: "Is a Chicano—or Black, or American Indian— REALLY an American? Then why doesn't he SPEAK like an American?" By their standards, of course, Mark Twain had no business letting the narrator of his greatest book speak in the vulgar uneducated English of a grade-school dropout, which obviously cannot be used to communicate anything to such educated persons as our cultural guardians.

2. See, for instance, Frank Lentricchia's brilliant discussion in *Ariel and the Police: Michel Foucault, William James, Wallace Stevens* (Madison: University of Wisconsin Press, 1988), pp. 3–27.

3. "Speaking" has been republished in Simon J. Ortiz, *Woven Stone* (Tucson: University of Arizona Press, 1992).

4. What I said was, "I *had* noticed that culture stops at the Hudson, but

I'm from Oklahoma—I'll bring some over to you, if Massachusetts Customs allow it."

5. Milton, it must be said, made no known protest against the slaughter by Oliver Cromwell's men of the Irish Catholic women, children, and men who surrendered the besieged towns of Drogheda and Wexford, not long before the massacre of Protestants in the Piedmont. What WE do is a military necessity; what THEY do is a massacre.

6. I have modernized spelling and punctuation of Milton's text. Though written in 1655, it was not published until 1673—a year before Milton died, by which time King Charles II was no longer trying to imprison or execute him for having helped, in 1649, to overthrow and execute Charles's father. In 1673, the sonnet would still wake echoes of the deadly Civil War of thirty years before, and its protest was highly relevant to the current political situation: Charles II was secretly Catholic and receiving illegal financial support from the French tyrant Louis XIV, while the English Parliament in 1673 would pass the Test Act by which both Catholics and Puritans were excluded from holding any civil or military office. Milton's protest against minority-bashing was thus published in a year when the restored English monarchy was conniving to make Catholicism the state religion and the restored English parliament was excluding both Catholics and Puritans from power.

7. A colleague I respect has suggested that however Frost treats women in the poem, he does patronize the birds by suggesting that since Eve arrived all bird-music has taken on a human oversound. It's a good point, worth raising with students in an American Indian Literature class—though in Indian stories the lines between bird and human run differently.

8. I used to associate this sonnet with Frost's lyric "Come In," in which he tells of passing along the edge of the woods at dusk, hearing from the woods a thrush's final song before dark, and of being tempted to go into the dark woods himself and "lament"—but he refuses the temptation, saying "No, I was out for stars, / I would not come in. / I meant not, even if asked, / And I hadn't been." I thought that in the lyric, printed not long after the death of Frost's wife, the bird sounded like the spirit of Frost's wife calling him to join her, a call which Frost, independent and skeptic to the last, held back from, both because he wanted more of life, being "out for stars," and because he rejected the thrush-call as inviting self-pity.

Recently, however, Michael Cornett has printed (*Papers in Language and Literature* 29, 4 [Fall 1993]: 417–35) a transcript of a 1955 broadcast by Frost in which Frost speaks of "Come In" as a *political* poem—the last kind of reading I would have given it. He presents it as a response to the despairing "America's finished" poetry that was being written in the 1930s. Could it make indirect reference to the poetry of Robinson Jeffers, say in such poems as "Shine, Perishing Republic"? Biographers might check dates and letters to look into the notion at least.

9. See "Two Riddles," *World Literature Today* 66, 2 (Spring 1992): 229.

10. Of course people *used* to treat jokes as more *like* poems, preferring old ones as best. But if I am wrong, if "explained" poems don't take effect, then why do we pay hundreds of thousands of teachers to explain poems to readers who supposedly can't figure them out? I wonder, though, if professionalizing poetry-teaching has herded poets toward sheer obscurity, driven ordinary readers away from poem-reading, and subsidized bad writing that needs explaining. Who knows, the same may be true of prose-writers—it certainly is true of legal statutes and lawyer-interpreters, and may be for novelists. The next step might be to mystify newspapers and require a degree in reading newspapers before the voting booth is made available. I bet George Will would like that—until he saw how the teachers were demystifying his columns.

11. "WAS poetics" of course means "White Anglo-Saxon poetics"—they would not be Protestant until Henry VIII wanted to kick Queen Catherine out of bed, at which time the poetics turned *WASP-ish.*

Source Acknowledgments

"Never Again Would Birds' Song Be the Same," from *The Poetry of Robert Frost*, edited by Edward Connery Lathem. Copyright 1942 by Robert Frost, © 1970 by Lesley Frost Ballantine, copyright © 1969 by Henry Holt & Co., Inc. Reprinted by permission of Henry Holt & Co., Inc. "Jacklight," from *Jacklight* by Louise Erdrich. © 1984 by Louise Erdrich. Used by permission of Henry Holt & Co., Inc. "I Expected My Blood and My Skin to Ripen," from *Voices from Wah'Kon-Tah; Contemporary Poetry of Native Americans*, edited by Robert K. Dodge and Joseph B. McCullough (New York: International Publishers, 1974). © 1974 by Wendy Rose; reprinted by permission. "Speaking," from *A Good Journey* by Simon Ortiz (Berkeley: Turtle Island). © 1977 by Simon Ortiz. Reprinted in *Woven Stone* (Tucson: University of Arizona Press, 1992). Reprinted by permission.

Index

About the Author

Carter Revard was born in the Osage Indian Agency town of Pawhuska, Oklahoma, in 1931, and grew up in the Buck Creek Valley twenty miles to the west. One of seven mixed-blood children, he completed his first eight grades in a one-room country school, working as school janitor, farm hand, and greyhound trainer through high school. He won a radio quiz scholarship to the University of Tulsa, was awarded a Rhodes Scholarship, and in 1952 was given his Osage name by his grandmother, Mrs. Josephine Jump, and the tribal elders. After taking a Ph.D. at Yale, he has taught at Amherst College, held visiting professorships at the University of Tulsa and University of Oklahoma, and currently teaches at Washington University, St. Louis. He has published essays on medieval English literature, the English language, and American Indian literature, and his poetry has appeared in numerous journals and anthologies and in three collections: *Ponca War Dancers* (1980) and *Cowboys and Indians, Christmas Shopping* (1992), both from Point Riders Press, and *An Eagle Nation* (University of Arizona Press, 1993). He is working on a new and selected gathering of poems, *Unzipping Angels*, while tracking down a fourteenth-century English scribe and his patrons, and may considerably improve the world if given half a chance and fewer distractions.